D1507842

STRANGERS SHOULD
NOT WHISPER

STRANGERS
SHOULD
NOT WHISPER

by

JAN-ALBERT GORIS

NEW YORK
L. B. FISCHER
1945

THIS IS A WARTIME BOOK. SIZE, WEIGHT
OF PAPER AND MARGINS HAVE BEEN
REDUCED TO CONSERVE MATERIAL
NECESSARY FOR THE WAR EFFORT.

MANUFACTURED IN THE UNITED STATES OF AMERICA
BY AMERICAN BOOK—STRATFORD PRESS, INC., NEW YORK
DESIGNED BY HERBERT CAHN

This book is for
LEONARDINE CANNON

By Way of Introduction

THE TITLE OF THIS BOOK IS A GENUINE WEST AFRICAN proverb, which the author did not invent for the occasion. It may be found in H. L. Mencken's *A New Dictionary of Quotations*. This proverb does not say explicitly that strangers are supposed to remain utterly silent, nor does it imply that they are required to shout their opinions. The understanding seems to be that if they pretend to say anything at all, they should try to make themselves audible.

The author of this book is a stranger in your midst. It has been his task since April, 1941, to keep the American public informed about what was happening in Belgium under the German occupation. He has done so mainly through the medium of a modest weekly publication, the official organ of the Belgian Government Information Center, called *News From Belgium*. It was distributed free to all those who showed sufficient interest in what was going on in Belgium and the Belgian Congo through the war. Of the first issues, 500 copies were printed; later on it reached a weekly circulation of 140,000. Spanish and Portuguese editions were published for Latin America.

A number of readers of *News From Belgium* insisted repeatedly that the editorial writings of the paper should be put between covers. This was done in *Belgium in Bondage* (L. B. Fischer, New York, 1943); it is done again in this book. Apart from answering the readers'

vii

prayer, there is another justification for this publication.

In the author's opinion, the best way in which strangers residing in any country may express their gratitude for the hospitality they enjoy is to speak their minds freely and frankly about the major problems which are common to their fatherland and the land of their exile. Therefore, besides performing his informatory task, the author has also tried to tell his public how his countrymen reacted or, if freedom of expression had been theirs, would have reacted on the major problems of the day and even on some which belong to all times.

In doing so he has tried to avoid the most dangerous pitfall of all political or semipolitical writing: a nationalist undercurrent of thought as contrasted with a sound national way of thinking.

Everybody is inclined to feel that his country is the best in the world, and everybody is perfectly right there, because, being a microcosm of the physical and intellectual components of his fatherland, except in rare cases, he will thrive better nowhere than in his natural physical and mental habitat. Imbued with an overt or secret sense of superiority, he will often be rash in his judgment when confronted with a country and a civilization different from his own.

As a rule, the United States receives unfair treatment from visitors from abroad who write about what they experienced here. Some express senseless, ecstatic admiration; some revert to a global rejection of American life and culture. Nearly all of them are extremely superficial in their appreciations. Some of them come here and, not caring to look around except through the binoculars of their preconceptions and prejudices, often heap ridicule

Among the West European nations, Belgium could serve as a good example of democratic spirit in action. Her reactions reflect with astounding accuracy the feelings of many of her small and larger neighbors. As an average European, the Belgian is indeed typical; his country and its political atmosphere constitute a fair testing ground for what goes on in the mind of Western Europe. Belgium may not always, nor even often, take the lead in matters vital to Europe and the world at large, but one can be sure that the stand she takes coincides most of the time with the position spontaneously taken by the average man in Western Europe.

This book contains a number of chapters about Belgium's resistance against German oppression in which the main characteristics of the Belgian people appear in bright evidence, about certain Belgians who belong in the spiritual landscape of America, or who should find their places in it; in the main it is the recording of the constant dialogue the author had with this country for several years, as a student in his youth, and in his official capacity since the war.

Recently, an American organization nervously expressed the desire that all European refugees should be shipped back to their countries post-haste. Even for reasons completely different from those inspired by their proposition, the idea seems excellent. Thousands of men and women who have learned to understand America and are able to interpret it intelligently and with grateful sympathy, would go back to their countries and tell their countrymen about the atmosphere of spiritual daring they experienced here, about the unbelievable physical courage of Americans even in peacetime, about a nation that believes in life and in the future to such an extent that, apparently, it is more afraid of halitosis than of death.

If this universe is really to become "one world," the role of these men and women will be a most important one, whether they stay here or go home. The Euro-American dialogue of the future will be conducted mainly by them. As a believer in the Atlantic community of nations, the author, conscious of his limitations but having fulfilled his Belgian mission to the best of his ability, fervently hopes that he had not only a right but even a duty to speak and not whisper above the bedlam which the conflicting passions of this global war have provoked.

J.-A. GORIS

Contents

III

SOME BELGIAN PEOPLE

IV

CHRONICLE OF OPPRESSION

V

BELGIAN "IMPERIALISM"?

VI

BELGIUM IN THE FUTURE

I
EUROPE AND
AMERICA

1.—What to Tell the Milkmaid?

WHEN THE FRENCH TRIED TO IMPRESS THE NORTH African Arabs with the marvels of modern machinery, airplanes and the like, the sons of the desert remained unmoved. When the French had really shown them the final achievement of mechanical ingenuity and asked for comment, the sheiks just nodded politely and said: "Why do you spend your precious time inventing contraptions to amuse people? Life is too short for that."

Do not blame the Arabs for that lack of appreciation of our mechanical age: they dispense with the trimmings around things, they know that you can't change the three basic events of life—birth, love and death. To a certain extent the people of Europe are also like that. We are told that a Normandy milkmaid went on milking her cow while all around her Yanks and Nazis were fighting in the meadow. A seven-year-old American girl, riding over a bridge, asked if it was riveted or welded; the Normandy milkmaid did not ask if the soldiers used bazookas or submachine guns, she went on about her usual business. If the Yanks tell her that the Empire State Building is that high, she will not be interested, but she will listen eagerly

3

if she is told what the milkmaid in Montana does on Sunday afternoon.

The trouble with the world (one of the troubles, of course) is that peoples do not know how to make conversation: as a rule they are boastful. The French say: we have the Eiffel Tower. The English say: we have the crown jewels in the Tower of London. In Baltimore they have the Duchess of Windsor's bathtub, and in Antwerp they have a shoulder bone of the giant who once ruled the city. It is a bone of a whale, but that doesn't matter. Every nation, every city seems to bring forward only those things which are exceptional and therefore not characteristic of its real existence, and the world is presented to us like a curiosity cabinet.

Something should be done about it: some way should be found so that the Americans who are swarming over Europe might forget about skyscrapers, ships built in the wink of an eye and airplanes that go faster than light and gossip. The Europeans should be told how America really lives.

They should know that the United States is an enormous but provincial country. That the *Penasco Valley News* reports not only world events but also informs its readers that Mrs. R. Waters has had her tonsils removed, that Esther Cartwright has the measles and Bobby Burns the mumps. That Joe Stillman was in town Tuesday selling hogs and that Lucius Hartford bought some flowery wallpaper to redecorate his house. They should be told that every well-to-do American family does not have a swimming pool, but that the youngsters go out to the old swimming hole and that every five years at least one of them gets drowned there.

They should hear about the American churches, not so much about the cathedrals and St. John the Divines as about the humble white wooden buildings with which every village is endowed. They should know that a sexton of the Congregational Church of Walla Walla is very much like the sexton of Bouillon. And they should be told that in every one of these houses of worship there is an old maid who plays an asthmatic organ while the dapper congregation remains consistently off-key. They should be informed that the pastor and the clergyman walk around in the village just like the curé, apparently idle and going nowhere in particular, but in fact navigating between the moral coral reefs of their flock and trying to improve whatever can be improved of their habits and morals. They should be told that the Evangelists in Iowa shout and yell at least as loud as the Redemptionists in Belgium, that a clergyman in Columbus is the spiritual replica of the clergyman in Hilversum. If possible, it should be withheld from them that New York policemen filing out of St. Patrick's walk down Fifth Avenue preceded by a majorette whose anatomy cannot be considered a well-guarded secret, but if need be they can always be told that strange lands have strange customs.

They should be told about the American village, about the drugstore, the social rendezvous of youth, about that single soda high-school youngsters sip with two straws, which becomes in their lives the equivalent of the cup Brangäne served Tristan and Isolde. They should know about the way the boy greets his girl friend when he takes her out the first time to a dance—that "Hi!" a masterpiece of understatement which can express as many shades of sentiment as a Chinese syllable is apt to have meanings.

They should know about the pink and light blue dresses the girls wear, baring lovely shoulders and still bony backs. They should hear about the chaperons and about the good-night and thank-you-so-much kiss, a mere formality, a receipt and a conclusion. They must hear about the square dances in the barns, not about the acrobatic feats of the Savoy in Harlem, but about the honest "swing-your-partner" procedure where the partner hesitates a little when confronted with a bulky female.

They should know that not all trains in America are manned by lewd Pullman porters ready to strangle girls in the lower berths, but that American trains look much like rolling maternity wards with uncounted thousands of babies who are going to meet their grandmas and grandpas. That in the stations, soldiers, as everywhere else, will whistle at the girl in the window or imitate successfully an appreciative wolf call.

They should know that schoolteachers here, as there, look painfully neat and resigned, that pale and bespectacled (rimless, of course) assistant librarians invariably wear flowery smocks which must prove to the world their tidiness but also their permanent longing for beauty.

They must be informed that all Americans do not play jazz from 8:00 A.M. till 12:00 P.M., although there are some of this kind, but that on summer nights they sit, in silent, devout rapture, thirty thousand of them, in open stadiums and listen to the noblest music man has written.

They should be told that an American park is like a European park, except for the presence of Mr. Baruch. That it is full of lovers, of gentle old folks, of children, of ice-cream vendors and of benevolent cops. That on Sunday afternoon people walk around in the parks in their best clothes, and girl friends photograph each other, standing with a sugary smile next to the biggest rose bush, as if there were any connection between their budding youth and the floral display.

Not all Americans, they should learn, spend their time commuting from Hollywood to Washington; and thousands of Italians in New York assert with pride that they have lived and stayed twenty or thirty years *"in questo blocco."* They should be told that they are not always chasing money, but that many of them stop working when they seem to have enough to subsist for a while and go out simply to enjoy that complete three-feature program the Declaration of Independence promised: life, liberty and a chance to happiness.

They should know that the great symbol of American democracy, the initial step on the road to felicity, the first comfort in all the so many dramas of life is that cup of coffee one offers to those rescued from the sea as well as to those who are saved from sin through the Salvation Army. Frenchmen will offer a glass of wine—it will look suspicious. Belgians will offer a glass of beer—it will be cool. Dutchmen will present tea—it will look like a dark and menacing brew, but nobody will be able to understand without comment what the American cup of coffee means.

They should know about the small American town at night, about the strange howl of the train when it hurries west or east, about the poolroom that is a place of perdition, about the diner where the sleepy waitress keeps up a motherly conversation with the soliloquizing drunk, about the lighted Christmas trees in front of the New England houses in the countryside, about the farmer who comes to town with his skinny wife and a carload of kids and, with muffled curses, repairs a punctured tire before driving home.

They should hear about the Middle West craftsman behind his glasses, as reliable and as conservative as a Dutch watchmaker, about the night watchman in the New Orleans warehouse, as philosophical and inarticulate as the old men who watched over the goods in the European harbors and who could at least report that something had been stolen, even if they were unable to prevent it.

They should hear about a *human* America, not about a race of supermen and glamor girls.

It is said of the Frenchmen that they are unhappy as soon as anybody does not want to kiss them on the lips; they want to be liked and even loved. Americans are a little bit like that, but it is far more difficult for them than for the French to accomplish that ambition. They are handicapped by their own enormous and fantastic achievements. Europeans sometimes have difficulty in discovering the man behind the powerful machine, and after all it is the man who counts. We do not like people for their greatness; we like them for their weaknesses. Caesar used to hide his baldness by wearing his laurels. It would be a good thing if the victorious American on European soil took off his laurels and showed himself as he is: a simple, likable human, the salt of this good, lovely, brave earth.

2.—*Introducing the Euro-American Homunculus*

"I'm a stranger here myself"

WE ARE ALL STRANGERS ON THIS EARTH, EACH AND every one of us. The woman facing us in the bus, loaded down with costume jewelry and looking through us into a vacuum, the man who sits next to us at the drugstore counter and has no elbow room to lift his cup of coffee, the clerk behind the counter with his green eyeshade and the stare of a panicky goldfish, the unreal-looking female who grabs our hat at the entrance of a restaurant; they are all strangers. They live in their own world, they fight for their own existence and rights, they have achieved for themselves an unstable equilibrium between their efforts and their needs and they refuse to be invaded, to permit the balance they have built up through so many years of toil and sacrifice to be endangered. Thus are we all because we are all alone, and as Arkel says in Maeterlinck's *Pelléas:* "The human soul is very silent."

But we do break this silence by tokens and smiles. From time to time we abandon our natural reserve. When we travel by train or by subway we may look at the child in his mother's lap and, seeing that he is healthy and eager, ignorant of the fact that children are bombed to pieces in London and Berlin, in Chungking and Cologne, we may smile on the child and the mother to inform her that we both know how frail life is and how much the infant has to learn before he will be as silent and reserved as we have become. Sharing a taxi with a stranger we will say, "My name is Jones," as if that declaration meant anything at all. Therefore, the gentleman from Boston who replied, "Mine is not," was perfectly right. He had learned nothing by our statement and refused to be invaded under false pretenses. But we can go further and volunteer the information that we hail from Oklahoma or from Oregon. Then we have advanced a great deal, we have conquered the first hedgerow of our partner's privacy, because nobody can with impunity be from any place on earth, nobody can deny that his home (he may love or loathe it) has affected his body, his speech, his thoughts. Nebraska is as much "a state of mind" as Virginia.

When at a quiz program a sailor, all set to answer the question: how many shoes there are in a pair, tells the quiz master that he comes from Maine, we all heartily applaud, but we would do the same if he were from Utah. Not for any special affection we have for the lobster-loving Mainites or the copper-smelting Utahans, but we have been given a clue to the privacy of another being, a small sesame to his treasure house, possibly what Ogden Nash's Venus calls "a key to his ignition."

According to general usage, there are strangers and "hopeless" strangers. When the common type of stranger arrives in a village, he is greeted with that title. Any man the townspeople have never seen before is saluted with that declaration of principle: "Hi, Stranger!" It marks a distance but at the same time it establishes a bridge which a few beers and a talk on the weather and the crops will allow us to cross. But a *hopeless* stranger is a man who cannot be anything else but that, who is condemned to be a stranger whatever happens, who definitely does not belong and never will.

Many a European refugee among you is that man. He may be willing to be one of you, but he cannot. He walks among you, he looks at you, you listen to his accent that sounds to you like a lisp or like a raucous rattle, that transforms a grown man into a callow youth and an adult woman into a sulky child, and you feel that he experiences America in a way different from yours, that the simplest and most usual gestures of life affect him in an unknown manner, that he is indeed a stranger without hope.

For four years now he has struggled with the 135,000,-000 Americans as Jacob fought with the angel. At the dawn of the new day, both were exhausted and neither had won, but the "hollow of Jacob's thigh" was out of joint. Thus it is also with Jacob, the refugee among you, for he did not come untouched out of the long mental ordeal of this war, and now that he sees the dawn of peace rising he understands what happened to him and he asks no more. He knows he can't go home again because, a stranger among you, he has become somewhat alien to his compatriots too. For they will discover in his eyes that carefully concealed smile when the significance of their quarrels or the ardor of their pursuits simply amuses him, although in the past he may have been one of the most ardent participants in their conflicts. For all time the hollow of his thigh is wounded.

If he were like that transparent glass figure of man exhibited at the World's Fair, one might see flowing through his veins everything European and everything American: the blue blood of an old aristocratic culture mixing with the carmine red of a young, vigorous race. He is not lost to Europe; he is not won to America: he is a new man, the Euro-American homunculus.

He is not easy to recognize. His disguise is subtle and elaborate. He hid or discarded his winged collars and his striped trousers, but he did not give up most of his sharp concepts or straight-lined ideas on the world and man. He may venture to wear one of those ties on which olive palm trees swing in the breeze on a canary-yellow background: it just proves that he is a good-natured humorist making an ultimate concession to the natives of this land, but inside he is all for conservative relations between classes and sexes, and Reno is anathema to him. He may give up politely kissing the ladies' hands, for Anita Loos has told him that although this practice is nice, a diamond bracelet lasts forever. After four years he may even say "Mac" to a chauffeur and "Babe" to a waitress, but he will fall in line when he meets the former president of the defunct audit chamber of a defunct kingdom and call him *"Monsieur l'Auditeur Général"* every other sentence. He breaks his European incognito ever so often, for he has adopted your cigarettes but not your ideas or your prejudices. Only the experienced observer notices his antics and comments: *"Connu, beau masque."*

Not a few Americans who came to Europe abandoned their own continent to find fulfillment of their personality in places which from a distance they would have considered dusty and uninteresting. They gave up some of the mechanical amenities of modern life for the advantage of being among people they considered endowed with that most precious gift, the art of living, which, after all, is a form of acceptance of death, a reconciliation with our unavoidable exit. These Americans felt that the Europeans, having devoted far more time to this matter than any among them could, were good to listen to and to imitate. That accounts for so many prominent voluntary American exiles. But also not a few Europeans have "resigned" from Europe after spending a number of years on those shores. They were not in quest of wisdom; they were the healthy outdoor type, the doers, those who felt that Europe as a dominant entity in the world was finished and that one should hitch one's star to the fastest wagon available, not to a Hungarian oxcart or to a Venetian gondola. They suffocated in Europe and they wanted their children to have some elbow room. The Euro-American homunculus does not belong to this group: he is bound to go back to his country and to become a missionary of everything American. He has been within your gates, he knows your strongholds and your camouflage. He has the password to your home. It is the same one Nero gave to his guards: "The best of mothers."

What can you expect from this man whose heart, for the rest of his life, will be a house divided? Will he sing your praise? Will he swoon with delight at the mere mention of Broadway, the Loop or Beacon Hill? It is not as simple as that: being a European, he will be critical, but being enamored of America, his brain will lose some of its edge. He will be just, he will try to be just.

The wonderful tales we hear about aviation and fast ships bringing all peoples together in a great brotherhood are plain balderdash. Most of the people everywhere in the world spend their whole lives within a few blocks; millions of the so-called "eminently migratory" Americans have never left their home state: only a very restricted number of persons are able to go to and fro between continents. A few thousand refugees spent four years on this continent. They hoped against hope in 1940, they lived only to see the curse of oppression lifted from their beloved homeland. Now they rise in the clear American morning, and every day they notice the dew of victory scintillating on the headlines. They still go around among you, but they think of their luggage. They are going home again, altered, wiser, better men.

They have a mission and they will fulfill it: to explain America to Europe, to tell the old continent that whatever happens on these shores, whatever violence might upset the social order, there is something indestructible here, something glorious and invigorating Europe needs, that Western civilization does not end at Cherbourg or at Brest, but that Europe and America are complementary entities, as inseparable and one as the Magdeburg hemispheres.

3.—*Europe Will Never Die*

THE DRY SOIL OF MESOPOTAMIA KEPT, FOR OUR MODERN curiosity, the tablets on which the overlords of Babylon wrote their cuneiform orders to their officers and to the keepers of their granaries, but it also preserved for us the many fragments of that oldest and most pessimistic of great epics, the Gilgamesh poem, which scarcely anybody reads and which is one of the most moving books man has ever written. Little more is left of the powerful empires those people built. It is enough. An empire has gone, a civilization has crumbled, but we reaped the crumbs.

In Central America the white man destroyed the ancient culture of the Mayas and the Aztecs. The jungle and the forests covered its pyramids, its huge statues of man-eating idols, its sun terraces and the highly colored pageant of Indian life, with its grimacing, inhuman heroes and cruel gods. Little is left of the Mexican and Peruvian civilization, little of it lives in us, but it keeps coming back all the time, and one day it may be a real part of our common cultural heritage.

There seem to be no lost cultures. Whenever man does something worth his while it is bound some day to flourish, to embellish and enrich the world and its inhabitants. We are told to weep over fallen empires and lost civilizations. Nobody should weep over an empire. It is a political structure and therefore a thing subject to changes and adaptable to circumstances. There are no lost civilizations. If they are of any significance, if they have any message at all, they spread out, they expand into less advanced territories; intellectual and cultural endosmosis is a constant and marvelous reality.

The smallest millinery shop in a Midwestern tank town will call itself The Bon Ton, as homage to the France of the seventeenth century, the culture of which dominated Europe. The politico will proclaim that he stands for the rights of "hoi polloi," and confess by those words our indebtedness to Greece for all our political concepts. France does not rule the continent any more, neither has Greece any great power, but the good they once did lives long after their moment of material supremacy is past.

For many decades prophets of gloom and doom have been busy predicting that Europe was going to die. All around us we hear that the British Empire is tottering, and people who otherwise would not even hurt a mosquito are indignant that it does not fall right away.

If the British Empire has to fall, it will do so for the good reason that when something has outlived its usefulness it withers away and decomposes, but a living body is able to adapt and transform itself, to survive by evolution. Before prophesying on that point one should be able to estimate to what extent that Empire lives in the heart of the members of the Commonwealth.

As for Europe, it has been solemnly casketed and buried by that scholarly German gravedigger Oswald Spengler, and, long before him, by quite a number of Americans who wrote on the subject, and implicitly by all the immigrants from Europe who turned their backs on that Asiatic peninsula and renounced her once and for all. For all of them Europe had died; they even refused to look back at her sickbed, but rushed to the wide-open arms of that wonderful stout lady in the nightgown who in New York's harbor proclaims:

> Give me your tired, your poor,
> Your huddled masses, yearning to breathe free. . . .

and whose sweet name is Liberty.

Now more than ever men think and say that Europe is done for, Europe is dying. Civil war has ravaged Spain, the greatest of all wars sweeps over the whole European continent, leaving only four steppingstones over that torrent of blood and horrors, Portugal, Switzerland, Sweden, and Eire. The loveliest monuments are demolished by only a few bombs, the great cities are laid waste, irreplaceable beauty goes up in smoke and ashes. That which made Europe so attractive to foreigners, its picturesque appeal, is rapidly disappearing. Tourists will not come any more except to visit the ruins. Europe is so prostrated that she will not recover. "Thus speaketh the fool in his ignorance."

Certainly Europe is ugly-looking; she is no longer the luscious beauty the mythical bull Jupiter carried away. Her looks are not so good. A few months before the war an American woman visited provincial England. She came back and wrote a book (most of them do, and some even do it well) in which she said that she had studied the English young people in the village pubs. She announced that they were physical wrecks and that they all had badly neglected teeth. She concluded that the English people would go under at the first attack.

Her appraisal of the situation is typical of that specific Greek trend of mind a great number of Americans have come to consider as an ideal—not to cultivate the excellence of the mind or the perfection of the body alone (except for women), but to require that man should have both and be as careful about conserving or improving his brains as his looks. If Socrates had been handsomer, he might not have been condemned to death. The good-looking man on this continent is always 50 per cent right. Europe is not good-looking any more, nor were the teeth of the young Englishmen, but the history of these last few years proves that both still can bite.

Europe will never die, for Europe is a powerhouse and a melting pot of spiritual values the like of which exists nowhere else. You can bring here the best of each country, and it is fortunate that you do, but for one generation at least it will be eccentric, foreign and accidental. Because a culture's greatness grows out of the apparent waste which accompanies it, because for every great painter it produces there have been hundreds of mediocre painters and thousands of week-end artists. For every great author there have been millions of passable, insignificant or silly books. For every cathedral built there have been erected thousands of annoying ogival monstrosities. You can derive great enjoyment from the isolated masterpiece, but to appreciate it to the full one must still hear in the background the rumbling echo of all the attempts that failed, of all the partial successes, of all the approximations and near-masterpieces.

In Europe alone do people have time to devote to all this. In Europe alone people do not believe that they have the right to be happy. They are sad with experience and therefore humble when confronted with real happiness. Their art, their culture, expresses their amazement that anybody on this earth could be happy for more than a few hours at a time. They are the professional pessimists in this world of ours, as Americans are the persistent optimists.

They may be reduced to a second-rate position, economically and politically; they never will be so reduced morally or spiritually, for every country in Europe has its word to say, in its own way. The statesmen of the early nineteenth century spoke of "the concert of nations," of "*le concert européen.*" They were right: the sound Europe makes is the sound of a concert, with its basses, its cellos, its flutes and its triangles. You need every one of them; none of them is useless. Europe's cultural history is much like Ravel's "Bolero": the melody is always the same, but each time it is repeated another instrument comes to the fore and interprets in its own way the basic motive. So through the ages every European country has in its turn dominated the concert and influenced all the others. That melody will never end.

It is Europe's task to tell the world that there comes an end to the sunniest day, that this lovely earth is a vale of tears, that the beauty and the beast both have to die an ugly death, that life is an interlude, an introduction and a trial. Those things should be said. Europe alone has pondered over them for centuries, and ever so often, in some obscure corner of that continent, somebody stands up, using perhaps a little-known language, and utters the same old truths with a new voice. It echoes all over the world.

Millions of people have died in Europe; millions have

been slaughtered. Those who escaped from that hell and witnessed the sufferings and crimes must have a message for the rest of the universe. It would be unbearable to think that the shouts of anguish and terror of the fourteen hundred Jews who were pushed into a synagogue in Lodz and burned alive there would not have an echo in the spiritual life of the world. It would be unbearable to think that out of the monstrous crimes committed by the Nazis there would be no flowering of mercy. The Spanish civil war gave us the fantastic story of the Toledo Alcazar: seldom have human greatness and human cruelty been demonstrated more vividly by both sides engaged in the fight. The history of Europe, old and new, is full of these incidents which tell us clearly to what depths we can descend, what heights we can reach.

Europe has been destroyed and maltreated a dozen times at least. It has always survived: it has even given birth to a new world which is now guiding and leading the peoples. It is diversified and rich; it is full of surprises and potentialities. It will not and cannot any more dominate the universe materially, but everywhere in the world people who want to "understand the reason of things," *"rerum cognoscere causas,"* will always listen to the lament from over the ocean, to the pathetic complaint of the victims as well as to that single great song of hope Europe produced, not the proclamation of a certainty but the expression of an age-old longing, Beethoven's "Hymn to Joy," which rose out of uncounted miseries and trials.

4.—*About Some European Ideology Bugs*

THE "NEW YORK HERALD TRIBUNE" ONCE PUBLISHED a cartoon entitled, "Our Bug Patrol," a product of the acid talent of "Ding," who very often defends with great energy the best and most worthy of causes. Since this drawing appeared in a leading newspaper, it may be assumed that it expressed the feelings and reactions of a representative segment of public opinion.

It was divided into four sections. The three upper ones showed the American Sanitation Services fighting with stern energy the yellow-fever mosquito, the European corn borer and the Japanese beetle. The lower section, designed as a contrast to the fierce resistance displayed by the entomology department, showed the American skyline adorned with a big poster, "Welcome to the U. S. A.," and a truly gruesome procession of unsavory germs and insects freely pouring into the United States under the general description: "All the Little Ideology Bugs from Europe." They were:

> Cheap Money
> Revolution
> Socialized Medicine

Communism
Marxism
Class Hatred, and
Socialized Industry.

This cartoon constituted not only a criticism of the internal policy of this country but was also an attack against Europe and things European. It attacked Europe in fact and by implication. Were those attacks justified, and was the picture the cartoon presented by any means complete and fair? There are reasons to doubt it.

The incidental accusation was that from Europe and Asia come some agricultural plagues: there is the Japanese beetle, the tropical mosquito and the nefarious European corn borer. These names do not mean much, for it is a well-known fact that nations are used to putting the blame for the plagues that befall them on other countries. Nobody accepts the idea that a plague could originate on one's own territory. In the terminology descriptive of certain diseases the French accuse the English and the English blame the French. If the European bugs eat the American corn, the so-called "Colorado beetle" eats the European potatoes long before the regular consumer has a chance at them. If the Japanese beetles eat your roses, the Japanese probably blame the ruin of their elm trees on an American insect. It does not mean anything; it is just a manifestation of national fetishism, and up to there the cartoon was harmless fun.

Is Europe's contribution to American life and culture limited, however, to this discouraging enumeration? The least one can say is that the list is incomplete and therefore incorrect.

A number of Americans object to "European ideologies." An ideology is a system or a group of ideas on a certain subject. Of course, only people who are terribly sure of themselves object *on principle* to ideologies. Every adult knows that an idea is more dangerous than a hand grenade, and cautious people stay away from both. However, most of us are familiar with the fact that nothing worth-while is accomplished in this world except through the force of ideas. We have to change them from time to time, and the United States would be a very backward country if the inhabitants had not been ready at all times to discard antiquated ideas for new and vigorous ones.

How dangerous and how European are the horrible bugs which march into the gates of God's Own Country, unhampered and full of ferocity?

The first one is Cheap Money. This is no place for a treatise on currency and money. Four hundred years ago, Sir Thomas Gresham, promenading in the first Exchange building the world ever saw, that of Antwerp, said some very wise things about good and bad, cheap and expensive money. We could let it go at that. But still it should be made clear that the cheapness of money is related to the standard of living and to international trade policy and that Europe hardly can be accused of having provoked a cheapness of exchange values in the United States. There is cheap coffee in Brazil sometimes. It is thrown into the sea. There is cheap wheat. It is burned. There are, or rather there were, even cheap pigs. They were killed. Only an autarkic conception of economy can produce the accusation or the apprehension that Europe is a center of monetary disease for the United States.

The second European bug that menaces this country is Revolution. Revolution against or for what? Just for the fun of revolution? Every foreigner entering this country is asked if he intends to overthrow the government by violent means. Even the Irish say no, and there is little record that foreigners ever took part in what in politics is called euphemistically "direct action." If it is true that President McKinley was killed by a man whose name does not sound exactly Anglo-Saxon, Czolgosz, Lincoln was killed by a genuine American.

Furthermore, a revolution is not in itself an objectionable thing: before enough people decide to risk their lives and try to depose by force of arms a government they don't like, there usually is a reason for such a move. The Boston Tea Party was a revolutionary gesture and what followed was a revolution. When Louis XVI heard that one of his most solid pieces of real estate, the Bastille, had been damaged, he exclaimed: "This is a revolt!" to which a sagacious courtier replied: "No, sire, it is a revolution." A revolt is usually a doomed revolutionary movement: a revolution has dignity and prospects; it expresses the will of the people. This country's existence is based on a revolution, and nobody has ever been ashamed of it. Of course revolution is an unpleasant procedure, just like an operation, but sometimes it has to be done.

European bug number three is Socialized Medicine. One of the most astonishing aspects of modern society is the fact that when a man is no longer in a position to earn his living, he is obliged to pay the technician who is supposed to restore him to health. At the very moment his economic position is weakest, he has to weaken it even more. We are told that the Chinese pay their doctors when they are well and stop paying them when they are sick, which is an excellent example of sound reasoning. The tendency to protect the workingman against the economic calamity of sickness is certainly a generous and excellent one. One of the few countries that has socialized medicine so far is Germany; most of the other European countries never wanted to go that far. They tried to prevent the doctors from exploiting the sick and they wanted to assure proper care to the poor. This usually resulted in a compromise between the state and the doctor, and the creation of an "order of doctors" which would establish an ethical code to which its members had to live up. If the discussion on this point was opened by the European countries, there is little reason to blame them. If the idea has been carried too far in the direction of complete state control, the blame may be laid to the Nazis. And the blame for the Nazis rests on all of us alike.

Then come up a couple of really horrible insects: Communism and Marxism. They are genuine European products—that nobody can deny—the one Russian, the other German. The American voter does not like them and proves his point by denying both theories any representation in his elected bodies.

A social theory, however explosive, offers little danger as long as it is confronted with a sane situation. Communism and Marxism are dissolvents of capitalist society: they are successful in those countries where capitalism has been narrow-minded, oppressive and aggressive. One should never condemn a theory of reform before looking at the situation to be reformed. There is evidently no social crime without punishment. If capitalist society exploits the worker, the pendulum movement of evolution will swing to the left, and one may feel that the reaction exceeds justice as far as the oppression did, but in the opposite direction. History drives a car on a straight road, correcting its course all the time. Both Communism and Marxism have evolved, have lost their original intransigency, because the organizations they opposed have also lost some of their objectionable characteristics. Both theories, however, have had a salutary influence in some sectors of society. The countries which deserved Communism or Marxism in its most pronounced form had it, but apparently there is little to justify these theories here and therefore to fear them is like tilting at windmills.

Bug number six is Class Hatred. One of the most wonderful pictures ever taken in America shows a group of wealthy, diamond-loaded and be-ermined society matrons walking into the Metropolitan Opera House on opening night. Tight-mouthed and a little grotesque, they carry into the sanctum on their decaying bodies their millions in jewelry. Looking at them stands a miserable woman, in a thin coat and evidently underfed. With an expression of indescribable hatred and contempt, she seems to spit at them, "Phooey!" That is class hatred in action, and who are we to find fault with it? As long as one class insults the other by an arrogant display of idle wealth, hatred is a corrective, an indispensable weapon, because people do not give up privileges freely. They stick to them, and only threats or fear induce them to relinquish their hold. Such is human nature, and that applies to the United States as well as to Europe. There is nothing specifically European there.

The last gruesome marcher in the parade is Socialized Industry. The two public utilities which in Belgium, for instance, are far superior to what America has to show are the postal service and the railroads. They are both run by the government and work out remarkably well. It will be advisable that in the world of the future a small number of vital industries should be state-controlled, because the peace of the world will depend on it. In time of emergency the government takes control of some industries, and every objective onlooker notices that this has to be done for the general good. After all, the state is a moralist and an arbiter; it knows that human nature is not spontaneously excellent, kind or generous, that private initiative does not always take into account the general welfare. Normally the moralist will be tempted to intervene every time harmony between the general welfare and private interests is upset.

On a healthy social body the bites of a few ideological mosquitoes can do no harm: only that body which welcomes sickness becomes sick. But social germs do not have to be imported; they will grow right where they find a favorable ground. Geography has little to do with it. Therefore, to represent Europe as a hotbed of explosive theories which would undermine the Union is an exaggeration and an inaccuracy.

As to the good things that have come from Europe to America, modesty forbids even an attempt to enumerate them. But those who walk through America's museums, who listen to concerts, who consult the libraries on any subject, who study American institutions, know that the huddled masses from abroad have brought to American culture and science a number of things for which this country always will be indebted to Europe.

II
MADNESS AND
METHOD

1.—*Babel Was a Charming Place*

SOME TIME AGO, MR. WINSTON CHURCHILL, WHO IS A master of language, a magician of the verb, expressed in terms devoid of ambiguity his complete sympathy for Basic English, much as John D. Rockefeller used to express his sympathy for bellboys and caddies to whom he handed out his celebrated shining dimes, one by one.

The reason behind Mr. Churchill's rather astonishing pronouncement seems to be that Basic English would be an easy way to spread the English language throughout the world with the result, it is hoped, of creating better understanding and closer co-operation between peoples.

Undoubtedly, all Europeans will applaud such good and noble intentions. We must try to understand each other, and a common language, even a crippled lingo like Basic English, would be a good thing.

The French-speaking people, however, protest. They are still conscious of the position the French language held up to the end of the nineteenth century in world affairs, in certain court circles and in intellectual life all over the globe. They defend French as the most logical language, the most rational, the best suited for juridical and philosophical discussions.

It seems to be an insoluble question, a matter of pure academic discussion. Some gentlemen prefer brunettes and some marry blondes. Every man speaking of his own language is apt to exalt it above all others, which is quite natural and logical.

Only during the Renaissance did people think that one should use a different language according to the occasion. One of the polyglot humanists pretended that German should be used to address horses and dogs, because it has a guttural sound which carries well. English should be used when drinking and making merry, French—of course. —was called for when courting, and Spanish was for all solemn and public occasions. The man who expressed this opinion was, naturally, a Spaniard.

A little later, Richard Carew (1605) wrote in his *Epistle on the Excellency of the English Tongue:* "The Italian is pleasant but without sinews, as a still reflecting water; the French, delicate, but even nice as a woman scarcely daring to open her lips for fear of marring her countenance; the Spanish, majestical but fulsome, running too much on the 'o' and terrible like the Devil in a play; the Dutch, manlike but withal very harsh, as one ready at every word to pick a quarrel."

It would be easy to find quotations from Dutchmen, Frenchmen or Italians to contradict all this.

The position of a living language in the world is, of course, always the result of two factors—its economic importance and the importance of the spiritual values it carries.

When the war is won, the English-speaking peoples will determine, willingly or not, the course of events in the greater part of the world, or at least they will pull heavily on the steering wheel. Their economic and political position will be such that hardly any statesman in the Western World will be allowed to ignore the English language completely without running the risk of endangering his country's interests. On the other hand, nobody really expects British and American statesmen to learn Bulgarian, Czech or Dutch, in order to understand better what is going on, but sensible Europeans will learn English, in order to explain Europe and to state its case as clearly as possible to the English-speaking world.

The importance of the French language in the postwar world is not to be measured by population figures; it will depend far more on the message that France has brought to the world in the past.

Among civilized people, anybody who purposely stays away from the French language impoverishes himself. It is not a question of grammar or syntax, it is not because a French sentence, to be really a French sentence, has to be limpid and crystalline; presumably one could write as clearly in Hottentot or in Persian, but language is not an end, it is a means, and there are some things that have been said only in a certain way in French, as there are others which have been expressed, for all time, in English or in German. The privileged position of French, however, is derived from the fact that French thought and sensibility have been so preponderant in European civilization, have taken such a tremendous part in molding the world's heart and mind that, even if France should be reduced to a third-rate political position, the radiation of its past and present intellectual greatness would prevail to a certain extent.

When the French poet, Charles Péguy, wrote the following sentence: "It will be very annoying, says God, when there are no more Frenchmen; well, there are things that I do and nobody will be there to understand them," people outside France were more amused than irritated. Whenever a nation gets possessive about the Lord, it sounds a little ridiculous but, anyway, there was a difference between the resounding proclamation of the Germans, *"Gott mit uns,"* and the way Péguy expressed approximately the same idea. His intentions were identical, but his manners were better.

The German refugee writers in this country have protested when humorous columnists have called the German language "a barbarous lingo," implying at the same time that English "is a sort of master tongue." This is, of course, poor taste, but in a way it is a part of American tradition. Mark Twain started the offensive when he wrote his well-known piece, "The Awful German Language."

No one who has ever had the privilege of reading Rainer Maria Rilke or Hugo von Hoffmansthal, and of enjoying the Mozartian sweetness and forcefulness of their verse, would take Mark Twain's statements at their face value, but the fact remains that most of the usual typical scientific or semiscientific writings in German force the Anglo-Saxon mind, as well as the Latin, to mental acrobatics which are completely foreign to them and which, to them, seem devoid of any utility at all. It is evident that the mental processes of a people are reflected in their language and nowhere else better. The analytical structure of English, the rational construction of French, are as distant from what Mark Twain rightly called "the parenthesis disease" of the German language, as the abysmal distance that separates European languages from the intellectual process which determines the characteristics of the Japanese language.

When some indignant columnists ask ironically: "Do we fight the German language?" or "Do we fight the Japanese language?" they do not state the case on a fair basis. We fight German psychology, we fight Japanese psychology, as reflected in the language of those countries.

Belgium, which has two language groups within its small boundaries, has a great deal of experience as far as language questions are concerned. Belgians know the psychological implications of the influence of one language on another and it may be worth while to see what they think of the proposition of spreading Basic English in the world. Learning a language, they feel, is not only a question of taking over a new vocabulary and saying *"eau"* instead of "water," or "bread" instead of *"brood."* A foreign language is like a foreign person; it brings into the home a number of ideas which are more or less alien to local traditions.

On a basis of proud nationalism, languages have been exalted the one above the other—a useless and futile proceeding. At the back of every language is a definite psychology, a tradition and a way of life. If the English-speaking peoples want to spread Anglo-Saxon ideas, likes and dislikes, throughout the world, they will scarcely attain that result through Basic English, a poor man's tongue. Simplicity in a language is not an asset, but poverty. The more nuances in a language the better the tongue. Those who try to convey their ideas and impressions through writing know perfectly well that there is no such thing as a synonym, there are only approximations, and there is only one word for every thing and every idea.

It is poor writing, for instance, when one speaks about "a woman of ill repute," when the Bible says clearly and without ambiguity "a whore." It is ridiculous and grotesque beyond description when one speaks, as did a group of Middle Western farmers in 1933, of "pigs and *enceinte* cows."

A language is a carrier of culture. It is unable to exercise its effects if it is reduced to a mere skeleton, if it is carried around as the intellectual carpetbag of a global moron.

If the Belgians who, through their geographic and economic position, are inclined to be polyglots, are told that one of the blessings of the postwar world will be the introduction into their cultural life of Basic English, they will no doubt have certain apprehensions. They are liable to ask: "Why don't we get more? Why don't we get the whole English language, which will allow us to acquire an intimate knowledge of the Anglo-Saxon mind? Why should we be put on an intellectual short allowance?" For the Belgians, like most European peoples, in their gratitude toward the English-speaking countries, will not be satisfied with the vocabulary of a taciturn hillbilly. They are apt to do far better. In the past some of them, renouncing their native Dutch, became great French writers; so did Chastellain in the fifteenth century and Verhaeren and Maeterlinck in the twentieth. Of course they used more than Basic French.

The important thing in the use of a language is not the language itself; it is what one has to say. There is little that is new in the world, but there are always new ways of stating eternal truths or ever-recurring delusions. Therefore it is imperative that one should have at one's disposal as delicate an instrument as possible. Basic English clearly does not claim to be such an instrument. On the contrary, it presents the danger of creating a linguistic class distinction and of encouraging the self-consciousness of persons of little intelligence and lazy memory.

On December 29, 1747, Lord Chesterfield, a man of keen wit and great experience in European affairs, wrote to his son: "Knowing any language imperfectly is very little better than not knowing it at all." It is highly probable that, with this remark in mind, some European writers after this war may, like Conrad, use English not in a clumsy and imperfect way, but in a manner that will introduce into English some of the characteristics and sensitivities of their own tongue, enriching it and giving it a new sonority.

2.—*One Story: Bataan and Louvain*

THE GERMANS COMMIT ATROCITIES IN EUROPE. SO DO the Japanese in Asia. Why do they behave like this? Apparently there is no excuse. There must be an explanation, however, which does not diminish the respective responsibilities of the culprits, but which may tell us where the roots of the evil are, so that in a common effort the free peoples of the world may in the future eradicate this growth of evil, or at least circumscribe it.

What is an atrocity? It is an enormous wickedness, an outrageous cruelty, an extremely heinous deed. The Latin adjective *ater,* from which it is derived, means black. For the Romans, an atrocity was a black deed, a fact to be considered a national calamity, and for many centuries *ater* and *atrox* have been used almost exclusively in conjunction with war and warlike horrors. Cicero called war a *"res scelesta, atrox, nefaria"*—"an accursed, atrocious and abominable thing."

It is scarcely believable that the lesson of the facts which have resulted in atrocious suffering for some members of mankind should be lost on the rest of the race of men. The Greek drama, which contains more solemn and solid human wisdom than any other writing, portrays almost without exception the most horrible happenings of the mythological world, from the incestuous horror of Oedipus to the nocturnal mass slaughter of the forty-nine husbands of the fifty daughters of Danaüs (Zeus must have blessed the one and only sentimental damsel who spared her groom). Why did the Greeks, who knew that wisdom consists essentially in avoiding excesses—and everyone should determine his individual measure—why did they indulge in such horrible spectacles, such monstrous atrocities? They wanted, as Aristotle puts it, to "effect through pity and terror the correction and refinement of our passions."

Through pity and terror! Those are the two sentiments which atrocities still evoke in all those who have already to a certain extent corrected and refined their passions. Of course, the story of the quite inhuman treatment in-

flicted by the Japanese on the American and Filipino prisoners resulted, on the part of most Americans, in very violent feelings. Such feelings are a safety valve and are
quite justified, but nowhere has the disclosure of these
horrible facts given rise to indiscriminate cries for repris-
als, or for any action that may be even remotely compared
to the level of beastliness the Japanese so naturally attained. It is even to be noted that only a week after the
Japanese atrocities were revealed, *Life* published a moving
photograph of a Nisei soldier who, fighting on Italian soil
in the American army, lost his eyesight.

To a foreign onlooker the reserve and dignity observed
by American public opinion on this occasion make a great
lesson, extremely comforting from the human standpoint. It shows that in times of crisis Americans know
how to correct and refine their own passions.

During the First World War a good deal of Allied
propaganda had an emotional bias. Use was made of emotional material as an incentive to patriotic indignation,
and in the madness of the hour some abuses were committed. Third-rate journalists turned out stories simplifying
the issues, dramatizing to the extreme conditions which
were already horrible enough, and sometimes even bluntly
inventing "facts." The most celebrated incident is the
story of the little girl whose hands had been chopped off
by the Germans. They had not done this, but they had
done far worse. On account of this one falsehood, the entire crime record of the Germans in 1914 was discredited,
and up to the revelation of the Japanese atrocities, the
very term "atrocity" was rarely used by the average American without a connotation of unbelief or a mild distrust.

Again, some people, giving free course to their imaginations, are getting out of hand. A widely circulated monthly brings us the story of a German woman who enters a maternity ward in Berlin. She sees a crucifix and says:

" 'Take that out of here. I do not want my son's eyes to rest on that Jew's face.' It was some time before the nurse and doctor could pacify her. Hours later, when she was returning to consciousness after the birth of her child, her eyes again turned to that spot on the wall, and she cried in the strength of fury, 'You have not removed it! Take that Jew out of here. My son's eyes must not rest on that Jew's face!' With a wry smile, the doctor approached the bed. 'Madam, you have had your wish. You have a son, but there is no need to remove the crucifix. Your son has been born blind.' "

In the etymological sense of the word this story is an atrocity tale. It is a story of extreme cruelty. But, furthermore, it is revolting and obviously false. It will do far more harm than good. This tale not only implies that the Lord objects to being called a Jew, which is rather amazing, but likens the Deity to a barbarous, ignominious scoundrel who would strike a newborn child blind, in order that its mother may be cured of her Hitlerism!

Those who write have a terrible responsibility in wartime. It is all too easy to stir people's emotion under the pretext of patriotism. When Nurse Edith Cavell died, her last words were, "Patriotism is not enough." Many people have carped about this phrase. They have explained that Miss Cavell referred to religion. In that supreme moment she may also have felt that above patriotism, even above religion and religions, there are a few universal human sentiments which must be respected if we are to live in a decent world. Those who invent atrocities or stories like the one cited above may consider themselves good patriots, but they are poor writers and poor men. Patriotism is certainly not enough.

The American public seems to have understood this perfectly well. Its reluctance to accept the news of atrocities in Europe, however painful for those who knew that these stories were true, was justified to an extent. When the unimpeachable testimonies of the victims of the Japanese in the Philippines were published, the reaction therefore was all the stronger. Some people said, "Please, don't tell us such things. They are too horrible. We should not dwell on the horrors of war, any more than we want to read the details of lust murders in our newspapers. Men behave sometimes in a beastly way, but that is an exception and it doesn't prove anything." This kind of response sounds strange to European ears. Europeans believe and have plenty of reasons to believe, notwithstanding Jean Jacques Rousseau, that man is not good. Therefore they are all too willing to accept atrocity stories. Some Americans, reflecting the basic optimism of American culture, believe that man is essentially good. If he goes wrong in such a terrible way, that is an accident. The explanation for that accident is now Nazism; in the Orient it is Japanese imperialism, or what-have-you. However, those who studied the events of the last war know that wanton cruelty, extreme wickedness, is the logical outcome of every philosophy based on the worship of force. The Japanese beat and killed American and Filipino prisoners. It is a shameful thing to do. The Germans in 1914 herded together hundreds of innocent civilians of Louvain, mostly priests, women and old men, in the railroad station at nightfall. All night long they kept them awake, to tell them with graphic gestures that they would be hanged or shot or beheaded. It was the particular pleasure of these pre-Nazis to frighten these people to death. At daybreak they were not executed, but were shoved on the road to Brussels. This is only a minor incident in a series of thousands of cruelties committed by the Germans, but it demonstrates the similarity of their technique to that applied by the Japanese.

They both believe that the only way to subdue a human being is to scare the daylights out of him. If he is of no further use, you kill him. So believes Hirohito, so believes Hitler, and so believed Wilhelm II.

Is there a way to avenge these horrible excesses? For civilized nations there is none. We can perhaps bring justice to bear on a few individuals who committed the crimes, although we shall be lucky if we find them. But we must punish the nation which has allowed such things to be done, whose moral standard has become so debased that such beastliness is a part of its war tactics. We must treat the vanquished as vanquished, and we should not consider them poor neurotics who, unfortunately for us, have escaped from the hands of their international wardens.

The martyrs of Bataan will watch our statesmen. The martyrs of Louvain, Visé, Tamines, Aerschot, and many other places, have been insulted in their graves because German propaganda has cast doubt on the story of their sufferings. In the invisible background of this war they stand side by side: those massacred at Deynze, at Rotterdam, at Lidice and at Bataan. They can't speak, but they judge us, you and me. They want to know if we will fail them again, as we foolishly did twenty-five years ago.

3.—"He Smites His Fellow Men and God"

SOME TIME AGO, AN "INQUIRING REPORTER" OF THE *Detroit Free Press* stopped four persons on the street, and asked them if they believed the stories they had heard about atrocities committed by the Axis in Europe and Asia. These four people, an office secretary, a housewife, a Navy Department expediter and a Navy materials inspector, gave about the same answer: "We don't." "The stories we hear now will be found to be false after the war." "We had better not believe any of the stories now in circulation." "They are at least fifty per cent false." "The tales are manufactured to keep us mad."

There is no reason to doubt the sincerity of these casual statements. Apparently they represent public opinion on the matter, as expressed in Detroit at West Lafayette and Griswold Streets.

Should we reject this phenomenon? Should we say: "After all, does it matter very much what people on West Lafayette and Griswold Streets, Detroit, think about events which occurred five thousand miles away, in countries with which these persons are probably not at all familiar? In a democracy, public opinion can be swayed one way or another with comparative ease, and what the average man knows and thinks doesn't count for much."

This would be the correct attitude to take if we believed in the policy the ostriches are supposed to follow when something unpleasant happens to them, but in the present state of the world, it becomes clearer and clearer that the influence of the little man, of the anonymous member of a community, is constantly acquiring increasing importance.

None of these four people claimed to be students of history, none of them has probably studied the records, none of them is an authority on the subject. Still, when asked for their opinion, they give it. They do not hesitate to oblige with their ideas, because they have the obscure feeling that the press and the radio have given them a fair picture of the problem under consideration. They may lack information and scientific training but, on the basis of other people's scientific study, they have acquired a moral judgment.

In this special case they are wrong, but their error can be explained. Like most Americans, they believe that they live in a "better" world, not the best one yet but, anyway, a definite improvement over the countries their forefathers left, either for political, religious or economic reasons. There they are right; there is little doubt that the new world they found here was in several respects far superior to the world they left behind. Human weakness has caused them to make some mistakes. We all occasionally behave like the dog in the Scriptures who returns to his vomit. For instance, they fled religious bigotry in France or in England, but they could not prevent themselves from hanging witches in Salem. They fled pauperism and industrial exploitation in Europe, but for some time they had sweatshops and ruthless trust management here too. But these were nothing but excrescences, incidents of growth, short reverses on the road to a better community of men. They never could destroy the American's conviction that this new world would not repeat the basic errors of the old one. Americans believe in human nature and feel that it is basically good.

They therefore rule out even the possibility of acts of utter and needless cruelty. It does not fit in with their idea of man. They know that some husbands kill their wives, and although this is a highly primitive and brutal thing to do, they can understand it as an attempt to solve a problem; but killing babes in arms, old people, nursing women, they refuse to believe in. They cannot see any motive behind it.

This attitude is puzzling to most Europeans. For after all, Europeans are experts on the matter of atrocities. They may not be so ready to give their opinion on a thousand subjects, but on the question of atrocities they can say: "On that day my father, a man of sixty, was shot on the market place of Aerschot," or: "My mother was bayonetted by drunken German soldiers on such a day and on such a street of Louvain," or: "My sisters and brothers were locked up in that cellar and the house set on fire. . . ." Unfortunately such stories could be told by the hundreds in Belgium after 1914. They were told by people who had experienced in their very marrow the brutality, the coarseness, the cruelty of the German hordes. These people did not speak very loud. They buried their dead, those who were attacked and afterward murdered, those who were burned in Tamines, in Visé, in Dinant, and for years they were unable to look at a German without feeling a deep and horrible disgust.

Of course, the thing to do would be to send an "inquiring reporter" to Belgium and have him ask the people he would meet on the Thienschestraat of Louvain, on the Kerkstraat of Aerschot or on the Grand' Rue of Dinant what they think about atrocities. This cannot be done for the moment, but fortunately something of the kind is happening.

With some astonishment the sociologists as well as the humorists—these functions should be combined—have found out that in the romantic mind of the general public, the war correspondent has become a figure of first importance. What a revenge! For once those who relate, who describe, who tell, outdistance the doers in the heart of the public. A great journalist in Europe is generally a man of wide knowledge and culture, who defends with logic and passion a certain political theory; he belongs to the genus Lippmanniensis. The reporter who simply relates what he has seen and experienced enjoys little consideration. The European reader distrusts fragmentary documentation; he wants a picture which includes all the outstanding features of an event. That a certain reporter saw something at one moment in a definite place does not seem conclusive to him. He suspects this reporter of selecting details according to his inclination and fancies. The American reporter enjoys a quite different reception. His testimony is accepted and taken seriously. He is an honest man. He is objective. He takes no part in what goes on around him, and he is as unemotional as an Anglo-Saxon can be—which is saying a great deal. His greatest quality, however, is that he is candid. He may even come from West Lafayette and Griswold Streets, but when he sees that the Naples post office is blown up by a time bomb, killing a hundred innocent people and dismembering children, he knows what he sees and reports it. One doesn't have to be able to quote Horace to understand what the Germans did in Naples.

For the education of the American public, which like all publics requires some education, it is a good thing that so many unbiased, candid men see with their own eyes what the Germans are capable of. One should read the description of the burning of the seven-hundred-year-old University of Naples, how the Germans compelled the inhabitants to watch the execution of an Italian sailor near by, how they poured gasoline on the university library and set it on fire, how they "punished" a town by burning its archives. It is said that AMG officials believe that the burning of the Naples University was part of a systematic plan to wreck all educational facilities in the occupied countries.

You may rest assured that an "inquiring reporter" would be able to find at some street corner of an American city a couple of people who would say: "The Germans don't destroy libraries! That's bunk! Just a tall tale!" The fact is that it is difficult to believe that anybody could be as repetitious as the Germans. They burned down the Louvain Library in 1914, they did so again in 1940, and in 1943 they burned down Naples University. Europeans are familiar with the German mentality of systematic thoroughness. They are not astonished at anything the Germans do, for they all know that little quatrain which a Dutch poet of the seventeenth century, Jacob Cats, wrote after careful observation and at a time when his country had never been at war with Germany:

> When the Hun is poor and down,
> He's the humblest man in town.
> But once he climbs and holds the rod
> He smites his fellow men and God.

4.—On Dying a Decent Death

THE NEWSREELS OF THE INVASION OF EUROPE HAVE shown us an Allied soldier killed at the very moment he sets his foot on the soil of France. He sprawls out over the fine white sand of the Normandy beach as if he were hugging the continent, but he is kissing the old earth of Europe and his own young life adieu. Few pictures could give us, the safely living, a more vivid image of what our responsibilities are at the moment and what they will be in the future. This boy—he may be an American, an Englishman, a Canadian or a Frenchman—died a decent, clean death. By doing so he made it immeasurably harder for each and every one of us to do the same.

To be born is no problem. Our first cries are not of moral pain but of physical reaction resulting from our first encounter with the outside world. The trouble is how to make a decent exit from this vale of tears. The Stoics spent most of their time educating people so that they could make what they modestly called "a reasonable exit." All over the world a great number of people and institutions devote their best efforts to telling us how to shed our earthly substance in good order and prepare for a better existence. A still greater number, of amateur standing, do the same: they are even more assertive and forceful because they speak only on their own account and authority. Then there are the poets whose task and calling it is to say that with all its setbacks and hardships life is a glorious adventure and death is a worthy dramatic conclusion to it. But notwithstanding all these road signs to our final destiny, all the often-contradictory information we receive on this essential problem, we are, all of us, constantly on the alert for a sign from above and beyond that will tell us the significance of and the reason for the fact that not all of us disappear from this earth because the physical mechanism that sustains us has worn out. The reason that not all of us die of old age, comforted by the memory of our achievements and the consoling smile of our children. The reason that thousands have to die in misery or are mown down by criminal hands.

Although most of us theoretically consider the abnormal prolongation of existence as a trying experience, according to the general consensus of opinion, to depart from life is an unpleasant and objectionable procedure. We object when we do not reach the number of years to which we consider ourselves normally entitled on this planet. They vary according to geography. Indians and Africans die earlier than Europeans and Americans, but everyone seems to feel himself entitled at least to the three score and ten years the Bible deems our appropriate schedule.

Since the war broke out, thousands, maybe millions of men have not reached that goal; they have died, and others will die in the prime of their youth. Of life they will not have known that moment of saturation of the heart, the senses and intelligence which is bound to come one day and which by its fullness and intensity over-whelms one with obscure fear and horrible apprehension. They will have known only the vague longings of youth, the impatience without fixed motive, the latent, generous ambitions. They will have looked at our society with the sharp, critical eyes of youth and found it wanting. They will have listened to their elders and have felt how a slight hesitation betrayed the uncertainty in their voices when they promised a better, peaceful world. They will have looked at woman and, confronted with her mystery and the sacred dignity of her task in the world, they will have been a little bewildered but completely conquered.

There is the story of the two Italians discussing life and death on Union Square—one expatiating on the misery of a death in battle contrasted with death at home, the other indifferent to the picture, always giving the same sad re-ply, the very résumé of his wisdom, stubbornly saying, "Die is-a die, die is-a die!" There is the story that came out of the last war about the American doughboys going over the top and their sergeant affectionately insulting them with the immortal and magnificent apostrophe, "Come on, you bastards, do you want to live forever?"

No, they did not, none of us does, but one of Marie Antoinette's ladies-in-waiting begged from the executioner who had everything ready: *"Encore une petite minute,*

Monsieur le bourreau!" "Just one little minute, mister
executioner." We do not want to waste our life, we want
it, short or long, to leave a moral, a lesson, an example.
Regardless of metaphysics, we want to make it a whole,
we have to finish it, and we know that we ourselves have
no right to decide on the moment of the exit.

Those who died on the Normandy beaches left no unfinished business behind. On their way over the choppy
Channel they may have thought about us. They may have
known that for some at least life goes on as usual, that
there are corners in the world the war has not affected,
that there are people who scarcely cared to read what
came after the headline, "Europe Invaded." They may
have discovered a hundred times that the war does not
change people but that in war their defects, like their virtues, become more apparent. They forgot all that, confronted as they were with a precise duty and an enormous
danger. They looked at the beach and remembered sunny
days when they ran along the fringe of the ocean, while
the evening sun projected their shadows on the sands as
if they were an antique frieze in motion. They reached the
beach and their ultimate destination: a well-spent life.

How are we to live up to their sacrifice? To the sacrifice of thousands of fighters on the front line and behind
that line, of those who died in the Ardennes woods hunted
down by the Nazis, of those who, having been symbols of
patriotism, died as hostages, of the millions of Jewish
martyrs, of those killed in mass murder and of those who
died from starvation. The last time we solemnly promised to "keep faith" with those who died. We have not
done so. When the war was over many people thought
that patriotism was enough. That if we defended sternly

and energetically our own rights, the rights of our country small or large, we should have done enough. It was not true. We are paying for it now. We have all thought that ardent nationalism was a sufficient basis for our conduct, a sure criterion of our actions. The present war must open our eyes to the greatness of what is before us: that is, a peace in which national interests will have to be sacrificed for the good of international understanding, the interests of big nations as well as of small ones. We have come so close together that the absolutism of nationalism has become obsolete and that we feel there are a number of things the fighting Allies have in common and should keep in common when this war is over.

Then only will it make sense that a boy from Indiana or from New Brunswick fell on the shore of a country he had never seen before, the language of which he did not know, and the customs of which were alien to him. Then only will it make sense that Belgian boys fought and fell in sight of St. Peter's dome, that others fell in the jungle of Eastern Ethiopia. We cannot go by these pictures and just say: the world is a bad proposition, there will always be wars and conflicts, let us make the most of it and let us pity the dead. For the moment will come sooner or later when we also shall close our ledger, shut our eyes, when our hand will slacken in the tender hand that holds it and, statesman or teacher, writer or laborer, we shall not be able to bear the memory of our weakness and our cowardice if we have not done to the full our duty as members of a peaceful world, if we have not contributed as voters, as public figures, as an individual moral force to the building of that house in which our children may live in peace.

5.—*"Der Weg Zurück"*

THE MOST HUMAN BOOK ABOUT THE FIRST WORLD WAR, *All Quiet on the Western Front,* was written by a German, E. M. Remarque. The most poignant novel about the immediate postwar years was written by the same author: it was called *Der Weg Zurück, The Road Back.* Because these books had a human quality which endeared them to the world at large, Hitler and his acolytes ordered them burned. No one in the New Reich should be permitted to infer that a German could not at any time be a superman or an ever-aggressive saber-rattler.

Remarque, however, had had a chance to tell the world how difficult it was for those boys of his generation who had left high school for the trenches, who had been confronted for months and even for years with hideous death, to find a place in peaceful society, to strip from themselves the cloak of heroism and to hand out groceries instead of grenades. This generation became one of desperadoes, of cynics, of disenchanted, revolutionary minds looking for a solution, any solution that would lend a significance to their sacrifices and the sufferings they had endured. To a certain extent the convulsions of postwar Germany were a result of this mood.

On the side of the victors things were not much better.

Ancient mythology, which is not merely a collection of fantastic tales, but which carries in its every detail a deep philosophical or moral meaning, tells us that every time Hercules had achieved one of his gigantic labors, he felt sad and melancholy, and regained his spirits only when a new deed called for his superhuman strength and daring. The chronicles of the beginning of the nineteenth century recount how the very young men who fought in the Napoleonic wars, who had conquered countries and empires, sat idle in the smoke-filled cafés, after Waterloo, playing dominoes all day long, unable to find or to take occupations which suited their sense of greatness and the magnitude of space to which they were accustomed. Like Baudelaire's albatross, their huge wings prevented them from walking on earth. In Great Britain, in France, after 1918 a similar atmosphere developed. Of course there were those who quickly returned to jobs which had been waiting for them and closed the war period like an unpleasant parenthesis in their lives, but there was a vast majority who had been uprooted not only socially but morally and mentally. They belonged to the Jazz Age, to "the Careless Twenties." They wanted to enjoy whatever they had missed in the war; they went to extremes, and the moralists of the age had an easy task censoring the antics of people who, having achieved victory and saved their lives and limbs, did not know exactly what to do with them. The peace had thrown them into an emotional vacuum which almost completely bewildered them.

Shall we go through the same moral depression when this war is over? Should we be alarmed and fear the peace as much as we hate the war? However repetitious life is, it seems that we do learn something, while the main characteristic of the Germans seems to be that they are unable to learn anything at all. The last war was conducted on a *dulce et decorum est pro patria mori* basis—it is a fine thing to die for one's fatherland, with fanfares and a constant exaltation of the soldier's profession as such. This one is based on a deep disgust for the whole business. It is not accepted as a glorious adventure, but as a repulsive job that has to be done. One must get it over with and forget about it as soon as possible, and one feels that it is far better to live for the country than to die for it. The outlook seems to be different and closer to reason.

When the last cannon shot is fired, when the last bomb is dropped, a great ominous silence will set in. There will of course be an outbreak of joy. Sociologists and statisticians are already calculating how many people will get drunk that day and how many accidents may happen. It does not matter very much; people will get drunk and accidents will happen and everything will be over in a jiffy. Then will come that dawn we hear so much about in the romantic movies. Those who break the ensuing silence will have a terrible responsibility. For they will, in every country, speak words which will determine the moral atmosphere of the world for many years. It is therefore exceedingly regrettable that statesmen already seem to be reverting to the Machiavellian conception of politics. It is not without horrible premonitions that we hear them declare that "this war is becoming less and less ideological." For this phrase implies that elementary forces bend the war that way, that there is nothing to be done about it and that an overruling fatality leads us. But the fact is that the statesmen themselves threaten to become less and less ideological. Now that victory is coming closer, they

have a constantly increasing tendency to show less interest
in what unites us than in what divides us, to revert to
nationalism and the *sacro egoismo* which is the policy and
the sempiternal excuse of narrow-minded jingoism.

If this war is not an ideological war, if we do not fight
for a set of ideas or if we fight less and less for them and
consequently more and more for interests, the thing to do
is to stop immediately or to leave the fighting to those
who like it. For every state is entitled to ask its citizens to
offer their lives for a cause and, fortunately, human nature
is generous enough to accept the fact that one may have to
die that others may live and enjoy some rights and privileges, but it would be rather difficult to convince people
that they should risk their hides in order that the rock of
Gibraltar might stay in British hands or so that the Belgians might continue to export cutlery to Bolivia. One remembers the chilling effect of the French pre-Quisling
slogan: "We don't want to die for Danzig." Dying for
Danzig was a *realistic* proposition; dying for democracy
and liberty is an *ideological* proposition. Nobody died for
Danzig, but lots of people are dying for an idea.

A lot will depend on what is said at the end of this war.
If the men who come back from the front are greeted by
the sly, calculating words of politicians who feel safe only
when they voice the local egoism of their people, who declare that all this dying and sacrifice had to happen only
for the sake of imports and exports, of banking interests
and the safeguarding of coupons and securities, then the
disgust and the revolt of the homecoming warrior will
know no bounds.

In his latest book, *Slavery and Freedom,* Nicolas
Berdyaev gives this magnificent warning: *"Everything*

which is not eternal is unendurable." It is quite certain that the horrors of contemporary history are due in large part to the overestimation of temporary advantages, to the violent negation of everything eternal. Nazism and Fascism were the direct opposites of permanent values, their sworn and deadly enemies. The application of their theories made life unendurable for millions of men.

It is imperative that the peace should not be made unendurable by pronouncements like those about the trend of the war which we have had to hear recently. When peace comes, every statesman in the Allied countries will be tempted to make declarations reflecting the basic impulse for self-preservation which dominates nations as well as individuals. He will be certain to find response and applause among his countrymen and will be praised by his foreign colleagues who have adopted the same attitude. It is possible for a plot of shortsighted egoisms to develop, for the ideological basis of the war to go to pieces. There is a great danger here, for if this happens the moral benefit of the most generous ardor and the noblest sacrifice will be lost, and we shall witness a new period of frantic greed, a boom of materialism, which will be the most certain prelude to greater horrors than those we see happening right now. *"Der Weg Zurück,"* the road back, should not this time lead to absurdities of the jazz age; it should be inspired by Berdyaev's profound warning that "Everything which is not eternal is unendurable."

6.—*Are European Nations Cynical?*

THERE SEEMS TO BE A WIDESPREAD BELIEF IN THIS COUN-
try that America is an idealistic nation and that all European countries must be accounted shrewd realists, if not
downright cynics. According to this school of thought,
America is not so anxious to protect her own interests as
she is desirous of securing the good of mankind as a
whole, while European nations, regardless of the rights of
their neighbors, are primarily concerned with their own
well-being.

If this were true, the moral standing of the United
States, compared with that of the rest of the world, would,
of course, be extremely high, and the satisfaction derived
from this fact would reflect favorably on each and every
one of the individuals belonging to such a nation.

This basic idea underlies a good deal of the recent postwar reasoning of certain geopoliticians and other world
planners. They feel that only that nation which, through
its undisputable moral position, stands above petty strife
and competition is entitled to rearrange the world for
others. With a broad gesture they sweep aside the individual claims of a number of European countries as ex-

pressions of plain selfishness; they refuse to cope with arguments based only, they are convinced, on narrow-minded egotism. If, by so doing, they behave like a stray bull in a china shop, they are able to point to predecessors of no mean standing. It should be remembered that Lloyd George became highly indignant at Versailles when his attention was drawn to the situation in the Banat of Temesvar. Who had ever heard of such a barbarous country, the name of which alone was an insult to the mellifluous Welsh tongue? Not many years ago, on September 21, 1938, Chamberlain, the man who sold out, spoke of "a quarrel in a faraway country, between people of whom we know nothing," meaning Czechoslovakia, which he could reach from London by plane in a few hours. All of which goes to prove that smaller nations, those who have no chance of belonging to the Big Four, Five or Six, or whatever you have, are an insult and a nuisance to some men for no other reason than that they exist and dare to want their share of the sun. In certain cases to ask for that share is regarded by some people, who don't even care to study the foundation of the claim, as evident proof of a lack of idealism on their part.

No one who has ever studied the elements making up American culture could deny the tremendous value of the idealistic motives in everyday life. It is quite certain that a kind of idealism permeates the best part of the intellectual life of this country and that, from there, it seeps down even into the most casual expression of the American way of life. To the European onlooker, a fundamental optimism is part of that idealistic philosophy. Even the most vulgar forms of smart salesmanship seem to stem from an idea which is familiar to every man and woman in this country—that the world is a good place, that people are nice and that evil is an accident and a result of poor digestion or an upset liver. When the cloakroom girl gives you a smile which a European woman would bestow only on her most intimate friends, when a restaurant hostess asks you in a low, velvety, houri voice, "How do *you* feel *tonight?*" as if you had been recovering from a deadly illness and this night was to be the night of all nights, it all seems to go back to the Rousseau conception that everybody is filled to the brim with kindness and sweetness, and that there is no other problem in the world but the social problem, which of course we shall solve before long.

There are, however, other signs of American idealism which are far more impressive: the spontaneous generosity of the average American man and woman, the eagerness and confidence with which they accept the cultural treasures of other parts of the world, their constant preoccupation with justice and moral principles rather than with practical solutions. If foreign observers are perturbed at times when confronted with the American scene, when they fail to understand what is going on, it is primarily due to the fact that there is often too great a gap between the principles proclaimed by individuals or contained in more or less official statements, and the application of those principles. To put it plainly without offense: it takes a great love for the United States and a profound knowledge of the dynamic forces of this country, not to be frightened to death by the distance between Lincoln's noble words on slavery and the sight of Negroes killed on the very steps of the city hall of a great American city. The remarkable fact is that, notwithstanding these horrors, the idealistic impulse of the American man is still a reality, that regardless of pitfalls his trend is decidedly upward.

But is the nation, therefore, in its political expression, to be regarded as idealistic? Is there such a thing as an idealistic government? There are governments which are peaceloving and unobtrusive, there are aggressive and imperialistic governments—imperialism being, after all, a form of idealism—but there is little evidence of the existence of an idealistic government. For primarily a government is and considers itself as constituted to safeguard the interests and foster the well-being of a definite number of people living within a given territory. Machiavelli has been blamed for introducing into politics a revolting cynicism. Of course, in his age, people cared little about the means employed if the end was achieved, but basically his ideas were exactly those of every government, namely: *salus populi suprema lex,* the good of the people is the supreme law. In international relations a government's first duty is to protect and defend its people. There, as everywhere else, it is bound by moral considerations. Although in their technique of documentation all governments use a number of means which in business or in personal relations would seem unfair, they bow to treaties, they fulfill obligations, they are not supposed to take undue advantage of another's weakness. But idealism supposes a readiness to sacrifice one's own good to help others, to suffer so as to alleviate others' suffering, to cut one's piece of pie in half and give one half away. In a democratic regime no body of voters would ever ratify such a proposal. Even when a thing like that seems to happen, behind the scenes one will find shrewd bargaining, camouflaged as a noble gesture. There are no idealistic governments, Q.E.D.

The providential function of the smaller countries, those who are unable to continue their existence without the goodwill of their neighbors, consists in stating the issue of morality before the world, in a permanent way. Even if they are born or raised as buffer states, for the sole purpose of avoiding constant friction between large countries, nobody openly questions their right to exist. When Germany invaded Belgium, it did not cynically declare that it wanted Belgium and was going to get it. No sooner had it reached its goal than it tried to prove, through documents allegedly discovered in Brussels and in France, that the Allies had planned to invade that country. Germany, in 1940 as in 1914, merely wanted to "prevent the Allies from committing a sin against international good behavior." This accusation, poor excuse as it was, was still an indirect homage paid to the sense of morality which should underlie international relations.

When one big country defeats another, morality is little involved. For instance, the Russo-Japanese war did not involve the world in a discussion of right or wrong; here was a fight between two apparently equal and logical adversaries, and no tears were shed for the loser. But the attack on and conquest of a small nation has always provoked a moral reaction. The small countries have no other means of defense but their belief in justice, their profound idealism.

They are not known to have ever provoked a war, but when attacked, their sufferings and sacrifices are in general proportionally greater than those of the big countries. In the First World War, the losses of the American Army were 8 per cent, in the Belgian Army they were 34.9 per cent, or nearly as high as the British loss of 35.8 per cent. The destruction wrought on a territory like Belgium, even compared to what happened in France, was enormous. On the other hand, the contributions which small countries have made and are still making to civilization are also proportionally greater than those of the more populous nations, the best proof being the list of Nobel Prize winners.

On the basis of what they are, on the merit of their contribution to the general war effort, the small nations have a right to speak. They are the guardians of the principles which should regulate and determine the world's conduct. When Haile Selassie addressed the League of Nations for the last time, he was defeated. He was no longer a sovereign, he was little more than a cumbersome souvenir. It is highly probable that in his empire democratic principles were not enforced with the utmost rigor, but the case of his country as such was clear and pure: in stating it he was the embodiment not of selfishness but of eternal principles. The present-day allies closed their ears to him, saying like the Athenians to Paul, "We will hear you some other day." The other day came and brought fire on Paris and London.

Cassandra was a bore, but she was right. It would have been easy for Agamemnon to slap her face and tell her to stop babbling, but the benefit of the prophecy would have been lost. We need Cassandras and we need small nations.

It seems to be the fate of the powerful that from time to time they become drunk with power—nations as well as men. He who has force is tempted to use it most of the time to the disadvantage of a less powerful neighbor. The

weak are there to remind the powerful that there is something besides force. The moral health of the world depends on them.

7.—*Idealists vs. Cynics*

RIGHT NOW THERE SEEM TO BE TWO KINDS OF PEOPLE
in the world, and it is a fair guess that there always have
been. The first think that we can improve on the world,
that we can make it a better place, which everybody agrees
it should be. They are called, ironically, idealists, dreamers or utopians. The others feel that we have to take this
globe and its inhabitants as they are; they have noticed
that it is a mess and see only two things for the serious-
minded person to do, either to jump through the window
or to accept this universe with all its shortcomings of
geography and psychology. They are called, politely, realists; smearingly, skeptics and, more commonly, cynics.

There are of course a number of people who may be
considered neither idealists nor cynics, who simply do not
care, but although they are numerous, they scarcely can
pretend to count. They are there just to be pushed around
or sometimes courted by the two active groups above mentioned. Possibly they got tired of making up their minds
between the antagonisms of their friendly brethren.

To make the picture complete it must be said that there

are traitors and fifth columnists in both camps: there are idealists who sometimes cannot resist the temptation to doubt the soundness of their stand and hopes, while there are also a number of cynics who in certain unguarded moments may reproach themselves for the attitude they have adopted, and who come very close to thinking that after all some of the dark brew we all are preparing for our offspring may become palatable.

The cynics usually say that the idealists are dangerous, the idealists claim that the cynics are without morals or generosity or vision. Nobody makes it quite clear who or what is menaced by the idealists; they are just naturally dangerous, as Hellenists are always "distinguished," virgins "modest," and old men "wise." Cynics are considered selfish and shortsighted; their picture is drawn clearly and in strong colors.

As a rule Americans range Europeans in the category of the cynics. Europeans are inclined to qualify the Americans as idealists. Woodrow Wilson was an idealist and Clemenceau was a cynic; therefore—so at least some people have it—Wilson was defeated and outsmarted by Clemenceau, that wicked old Frenchman. The moral of the story is that Americans, confronted with Europeans, are apt to be suckers, schlemiels, or "innocents." Such is the rather widespread belief.

We are told that Mr. Santayana, liberated in Rome, lives so far away from his age that he can look on this war with a detached view. He is a philosopher. There are very few of them left in this world, and it takes a great effort of sentimental absenteeism to be able to look at the coming battle of idealists and cynics with an objective mind. For all the signs point to the fact that both groups

are marshaling their forces, lining up their arguments
and inspecting their arsenals of insults and derogatory
adjectives.

At the moment the preliminary scrambles between idealists and cynics center around the policy of the Allied Nations and especially of the United States and Great Britain
with regard to the attitude toward native Fascists in the
liberated territories. The cynics applaud the many blunders already made and reason approximately as follows:
When we march into a liberated town we want order;
that means that the telephones must function, sewage
must be carted away, streetcars must run and there must
be food. You can obtain anything from people who are
well fed and clothed. If you are able to reopen a synagogue in the bargain, do so; it makes a wonderful story
for the newspaper boys. Bring life back to the city. Should
you have to use a Fascist, semi- or philo-Fascist, do not
hesitate. If he is a Prince So-and-So, everybody will admit
him; princes can't go wrong. The future will take care of
the rest, and Mussolini—he may have been a son of a
female dog, but he made the trains run on schedule.

The idealists, impenitent as they are, say: We come to
liberate people; that means not their bodies alone, but
their spirit. Thousands of these people have given their
lives that the spirit may be free. They could have had telephones and butter and first-class tickets on the railroad,
but they did not like the people who dispensed those
favors, and they died rather than accept an "Order" based
on tyranny, murder and falsehood. These idealists hold
that there is something more important than existence,
and that is a decent existence. They feel that any man
who has surrendered to the Nazi or Fascist ideology has

become a danger to the community of nations and has at least made himself useless for the future. These idealists are considered fanatics, because with a clear purpose they want only one thing and they want it completely. Of course, in modern society one should not be fanatic. One should leave that to the dervishes and the fakirs but, all things considered, Washington was a fanatic and Lincoln was one, so was Bolivar and so was Kruger. All of these men wanted something very strongly, without compromise or "arrangements." We therefore honor them greatly. It seems, however, that such fanaticism is all right in the past but objectionable in the present.

The issue involved in the quarrel about the use to be made of former Fascists and Nazis transcends the details of persons and locations. The European underground knows that very well. The clandestine papers in Belgium and elsewhere have expressed themselves on that point: they know that Fascism and Nazism are not exclusively Italian or German, that there are Fascists in every one of the occupied countries, as there are in the Allied countries. They know that Fascism and Nazism (a Fascism with the addition of anti-Semitism) are not only a political creed but are really a *Weltanschauung,* a philosophy of life, literally a vision of the world. The Nazis have proclaimed that ever so often.

Nazism and Fascism pretend to change the whole man, and they certainly do, because they take away from him the quality of mercy, and encourage in him all that is primitive and brutal. Already in the last war the élite of the German army was impregnated with these ideas. General and philosopher looked scientifically at the world: they felt that natural selection operates by an interspecific struggle or lethal competition for food, space and opportunity to procreate, by the intraspecific struggle of individuals of the same species, which is a result of overproduction due to geometrically progressive multiplication, and by the constant struggle of individuals and species against the atmosphere and climatic dangers. The biologists acknowledge these facts, but observe that in every species a certain amount of mutual aid or altruism is discernible, the highest being present among men. The German natural philosophers denied that thirty years ago, just as Hitler and his followers deny it now: they saw no solution but brute force.

In every country in the world, feudal, Fascist or democratic, there have always been a number of people who, out of principle, or most of the time out of plain egoism, believed in nothing else but force. Therefore we invented laws to keep them in check. Fascism, however, will not perish. It will die as a political structure, as an organized body; it will not perish as an idea, because it corresponds to the vilest but most widespread defect of human nature, egoism. The world will be menaced by it ever so often. It will be rampant and latent. It will never die, because it lives in the heart and the mind of those who anywhere in the world exploit people, in the mind of the roadhog as well as in the mind of the brute who shoves you off the sidewalk. It is a human crime which has been glorified and dictionarized, nothing more.

Say the cynics: We grant you all that. Fascism is a state of mind and therefore it is human. You have to accept it as fact. You might as well make the best of it. There will always be people who prefer to use a gun rather than an affidavit to obtain what they want. Do the same and natural selection will do the rest. Look at yourselves, idealists and crusaders! Are you going to divide the world into two clear-cut sections, the region of the good people who are all lambs and doves and the region of the bad people who are all wolves and hawks? Ridiculous!

To which we will answer that we fully realize that among the sheep there will be a few wolves and among the wolves a few lambs, but that we will do our utmost to get rid of those people amongst us who have felt and acted as if might ought to be right. We know very well that all over Europe thousands of philo-Fascists are hastily preparing double files to prove that they were at heart good fellows, although they wore the party button. Industrialists who got millions out of their collaboration with the Nazis give a handful of dollars to a few boys who want to go to London to join their national armies of liberation, proclaiming the patriotism of their patron. It will be to no avail. They will be weeded out. They have to be driven from their offices, out of the sight of the honest people. Westbrook Pegler has openly pleaded the cause of those people who collaborated "to avoid anything worse." We do not care for these men, for we know that in every country in Europe under the Nazis there were thousands and thousands of people who did not collaborate, who lost their jobs, their freedom, their lives, just for the pleasure of saying "No" to the *Herrenvolk*. These people will be the salt of the new earth. We do not need the others, even if they know the local telephone numbers by heart, even if they are able to state the size of every sewage pipe in town. Because we have one fanatical belief: that if there is any chance at all to make this world livable, it is by cutting off the dead branches so that the tree may grow, and we consider as dead branches all those who to any extent have at one time renounced that greatest of all treasures, human kindness, for the teachings that were put in practice for the first time by Cain and—let us hope—for the last time by Hitler and his henchmen.

8.—A "Reasonable" Peace?

THE POPE HAS SPOKEN TO THE WORLD. THE SPIRITUAL authority with which he is invested, the weight his words carry with millions of Catholics in both hemispheres, make his statements and his admonitions important. More than anybody else in the world, the Pope has the advantage of knowing what is happening and of looking at the political situation with detachment and from a standpoint devoid of partisan influence.

In matters of politics the Pope has never claimed infallibility. Although well informed about facts, he may err in judgment, even in tactics. He was seriously and rightly perturbed about the fate of Rome, but his attitude toward damage which might be done to the city was clearly out of proportion to what an average Catholic may feel about it. He who would hurt Rome "would be guilty of matricide in the eyes of the civilized world and in the eternal judgments of God." Charles V did so, and he was a great

Catholic Emperor, stern enemy of the Protestants. Among the sovereigns of Europe, he was one of the greatest defenders of the Catholic faith.

It is reported from Belgium that the curé of a small village in the Ardennes who wanted to reassure his flock about the fate of Rome and its repercussion on the future of the Catholic Church, said in his sermon that after all he cared little "if a few old buildings went to shambles." That was of course an extreme view, expressed in a rather blunt phrase, but basically this backwoods curé had a clear view of the question. In the two last centuries, men have indeed come to associate ideas far too much with their material symbols, with their localization. A novel of the sixteenth century is little concerned with surroundings, commits anachronisms with nonchalance and sticks to the essential thing: the story and the moral of the story. In these times of hasty and sloppy writing we have to dress a story all up to make it acceptable: we employ atmospheric trimmings and circumstantial descriptions. A philosophy, a faith, should be and is above localization. If it really needs a geographic location in order to survive, it cannot be very significant. Not long ago we heard that a devout pilgrim had inadvertently vomited on the holy stone in the Kaba of Mecca. He was executed, for the Mohammedans consider such a sacrilege punishable only by death. For them it was obviously worse than matricide. In the civilized world nearly everybody was on the side of the unfortunate pilgrim who died on account of his weak stomach.

Guernica in Spain was a holy town to the people of the region. It was leveled by German airplanes: the faith of the loyalist Spaniards, however, did not die with it.

Therefore the future of Catholicism was not at stake if St. Peter's Church had crumbled, or if the Colosseum had been destroyed. Both are shrines, the one of impressive grandeur, the other a witness to uncounted martyrdoms. But nobody needs them to believe in the metaphysical teaching of the Church. They are not indispensable, and their destruction would no more have been matricide than the demolition of the Houses of Parliament in London. Christendom is not a real-estate proposition: it is a faith which can live detached from archeology and which, in great measure, alas, lives detached even from art. Although nobody could have witnessed with indifference the disappearance of Rome or part of it, although nobody who knows the irresistible loveliness of even the smallest Italian town could have seen it destroyed without a pang, to have applied the term of matricide to such a possible event was mere rhetoric. About two hundred years ago Morosini shelled the Parthenon, which in the mind of every civilized human being, regardless of his denomination, is at least as magnificent a symbol of human greatness as some baroque parish church of Rome: the eternal spirit of Greece has not died. It is still vivid, it inspires us and nourishes us as well as the Christian idea. The Germans can take the whole Acropolis home and ship it to Berchtesgaden, but we shall still have the immortal words Socrates spoke after he had drunk the hemlock.

In another part of his speech the Pope pleaded for "a reasonable peace"; he seemed to be opposed to a "full victory." Since the tide of war had turned, that could only have meant that we should "talk" with the Germans. The Pope has expressed very often and very clearly his moral objections to Nazism: as a moral authority deeply concerned with the good of humanity, he wanted to see the war end as soon as possible. We have all felt like that. The Pope said that the thesis of "full victory or complete destruction acts as a stimulus" on the resistance of the losing side. There may be some truth in it: it may be that the Nazis, who know that their game is up, rather than throw themselves on the mercy of the victor, will prefer to fight for their jobs, their concentration camps and their extra ration points to the bitter end. But could this be a reason for the Allies to stop on their way to victory? Scarcely. If, at a boxing match, the manager of the challenger came up to the other fighter and said, "Now look, my man is going to fight hard, he won't give in till he is beaten," the other fighter would just lift his eyebrows in astonishment and go on knocking the daylights out of his opponent.

Of course—as the French say—a comparison is not a proof, but everybody who has lived through Europe's history for the last decades knows that there is no "reasonable peace" to be had from the Germans. They have never been "reasonable." Chamberlain "reasoned" with them, Daladier "reasoned" with them. Everybody, confident that the Germans must possess that wonderful quality of reasonableness, reasoned with them: the result was the Blitzkrieg. Germany is a great power. It is a rich country, located in the center of Europe. It can exist on a nearly autarkic basis; it can afford to lose several million men. When the war is over, it will have the physically strongest, best conditioned manhood in Europe, all its neighbors having been systematically weakened. If Germany gets a "reasonable peace" now, in a very few years it will assault Europe again, and might be victorious. In the case of Germany, what does reason command? To hold the country down physically, to prevent it from doing harm. The methods of ensuring that result are many; the basic aim can be only that simple one.

There is only a slight chance that Germany might be curable. Let us try it, but not by giving the Germans a free hand in their own affairs. Let them be on parole, but carefully watched. Since 1900 we have been waiting for one "reasonable" gesture from the Reich: we have seen nothing but bravadoccio and crime. How could we expect reason now? We remember that the whole campaign of national revival inspired by Hitler started on the premise that Germany had not been defeated in 1914. Germany cannot be defeated, according to German thought. All the rest of their reasoning is based on that: their brutality, their pretentiousness, their ambitions are based on that presumption.

The decision now is up to them: they are encaged in their fortress. If they have any reason left, this is the time to speak out and say, "We are licked, let us talk." But if they prefer to be completely "destroyed," it is up to them. If they prefer their party buttons, their SS and SA, their *Parademarschen* and the poor grammar of *Mein Kampf* to very existence, well, let them take the chance and bear the results of their folly.

There is in this war but one alternative: either Germany in a suicidal obstinacy destroys itself by resisting to the limit, or it recognizes its desperate situation and does what the good loser has to do. But as soon as one supposes for a moment that the Allies could "talk" to that scum of the earth which rules Germany now and "talk reason" with them, one has taken the first step on the road to the third World War, which will be bigger and better than anything we have seen so far. It seems scarcely possible that human folly could be so great!

9.—Does the Cow Give Milk? No!

DOES THE COW GIVE MILK? NO, YOU HAVE TO TAKE IT away from her. . . . Such is the wisdom of a radio wit, and it might well be applied on many other occasions. For instance, does peace give prosperity? Not at all. You have to go and get it. India was at peace when millions died of famine, China was at peace when floods devastated enormous parts of her territory, America was not at war when four hundred thousand impoverished farmers from Oklahoma and Arkansas started a courageous but lamentable trek to the West.

Peace is not enough, for we have been given this world in bulk. Few things are in their right place, or rather few people are; the most precious things are hidden in caves and underground. The biggest fishes stay far away from the shore and the best pheasant hide deep in the woods. In order to live we have to take away the hen from the cock, the male sole from the female sole, and if milady needs a bag in *veau mort né* we go so far as to kill the calf in the cow. We are really great ones for getting things. The reason, of course, being that nobody but our mother gives us anything free and pure, providing that even she does not prefer to serve us pasteurized milk.

There is, however, one thing which has been given to us, unequally distributed for sure, but still given: that is the gray matter of the mind. Since nature plays hide and seek with her treasures, we were given brains to outsmart her. But there persists among humans a vague idea that if we behave, if we do not cut each other's throats or break into Mrs. Vanderbilt's dining room uninvited, if we do not spit in the collection plate at church or try to use a French sou in the subway instead of the nickel Mr. La Guardia requires, we are entitled to a living, and even a good one. That persistent dream of permanent prosperity has been the theme of many a great writer and painter. Breughel, the most human of all Flemish painters, has given us a picture of the land of plenty where tenderly cooked chickens fly into the mouths of well-fed loafers, where soft-boiled eggs walk around on little legs to be of service to those who have an urge to such a breakfast. The Roman populace required bread and circuses; Breughel's loafers seem to be entirely satisfied with food and plenty of sleep. There is not even a woman around in this land of plenty—which after all may be a sign of great wisdom.

Nowadays we want our dreamlands to be more complicated. They must be like one of those wonderful postwar gadgets one reads so much about but never sees. They must be streamlined and elastic to fit everybody. Of course, for the benefit of the public at large the issues are simplified. Regardless of the fact that Hottentots probably prefer palm wine, they are promised a pint of milk every day. The phrase is used ironically, which is a heartless thing to do and is destined to provoke the jealousy of people who up to now have not always been sure of having that very pint at hand.

Hitler divided the world between the "haves" and the "have-nots." Strangely enough, having nothing, he still had enough to overrun Europe and keep the world at bay for several years. Which proves that not all those who pretend to be without means are really so dispossessed. Furthermore, it is a well-known fact that millionaires serve themselves best at a free buffet and take another cigar home at the end of the dinner. All of which goes to show that the distribution of goods after the war on an equal basis so as to assure prosperity to everyone will be a hell of a job.

The Belgians are known as a realistic people. They have never expected anybody to make them completely happy without effort on their part. They are like that lady who was so very old that she became an atheist. They have seen so many unpleasant things, they have been cheated so often, that they doubt even Santa Claus. What do they expect from the postwar era? Unmixed economic, political and social bliss? A land of milk and honey, of free frosted coffees and Coca Colas?

There are two kinds of Belgians right now: a majority inside the country, a minority outside. The 8,360,000 Belgians inside Belgium were handicapped in their expression by the fact that although they had a vigorous underground press, it was difficult for them to keep in contact with public opinion. No general exchange of ideas was possible. What we know of their feelings is a sum total of the sentiments expressed by the organs of a number of more or less isolated, smaller or larger groups.

On the other hand, there were the Belgians in the free countries, grouped around their government, unanimously loyal to it and operating in close collaboration with it. They were of course separated from their home country, but they knew it and they loved it dearly. Many of them were in exile for the second time in their lives, so that they were familiar with what their countrymen inside Belgium had to expect.

The Belgians in the occupied territory knew that liberation would come, but they were convinced that it would be costly. It already has been, in lives and material. The maps of bombings in Europe show that the heaviest assaults, except for certain German regions, were delivered in Belgium: a great number of cities suffered heavily. One can't drop a bomb on Belgium anywhere without killing civilians: there are seven hundred and ten of them per square mile.

The Belgians knew that they would have this price to pay. They plan to rebuild. They were already trying to do so when the ruins of 1940 were still smoldering, for like human folly, human energy is boundless. The Germans refused them the means of reconstruction, and only work useful to the Army Command could be undertaken. The war had shown them that emergencies could come up which created misunderstandings extremely dangerous for the country's safety and for which no provision was made in their laws. Therefore Belgians under the occupation spent their time redrafting their constitution, which was written one hundred and fourteen years ago and has been little changed since. They also made other plans. Political parties drew up new schemes, and the Socialist underground printed its postwar program. It is no utopian proclamation, promising chicken every day and caviar on Sunday, but a piece of realistic writing, going into a great number of details as far as the social and economic order is concerned. It is progressive without being revolutionary and appears to be the result of a thorough study of Belgian conditions. Other political groups have developed similar well-laid-out plans.

In Great Britain the Belgian government in exile (which has a branch office in New York) was the first to establish at the beginning of 1941 a "Commission for the Study of Postwar Problems," under the presidency of Mr. Paul van Zeeland, former Prime Minister of Belgium. It is an advisory board comparable to the National Resources Planning Board of the United States. It has a consultative function and limits its activities to study and research. The work of this Commission is based on all the academic findings, knowledge or experience available and has already accomplished a very considerable amount of work. When plans are sufficiently advanced, they are submitted to the government. Already a number of them have been adopted and transformed into legislative form. The Belgian government in London kept the Belgian population informed of these plans and of the solutions adopted, so that when the day of complete liberation came those in responsible positions might be prepared to carry them out. The Belgians therefore know already the outlines of their future economic, social and political existence: they are aware of the fact that these outlines have been drawn by men who had at their disposal not only their profound knowledge of the home country but who were fortunate enough to be able to study the Anglo-Saxon world and to meet on intimate terms most of the men who tomorrow will play decisive roles in the universe at peace. The Belgians inside Belgium had little or no knowledge of the economic and social happenings and trends in the free world. The refugees in Great Britain or the United States had ample opportunity to study the signs of the future.

When peace comes again in Belgium, everything will be ready to make it a better, happier country. Those who had the foresight to do the planning and to examine the possibilities of their country in the postwar world, on a practical basis, not in the spirit of a utopian Eldorado, will be entitled to the gratitude of the nation and, in so far as these plans will assure peaceful transitions, of the world.

10.—"They Do Those Things So Well in France"

THIRTY-EIGHT PER CENT OF THE 8,360,000 BELGIANS speak no language but French. In addition, 12 per cent of them are able to understand and to speak it, so that exactly half of the Belgian population comes in close contact with French civilization, and at least 38 per cent of them depend for a good part of their intellectual life on what France has to offer. It should not therefore seem astonishing if France's fate and fortune aroused great interest among the Belgians inside the occupied territory as well as among the approximately 100,000 Belgians in exile throughout the free world.

For a relatively small country like Belgium, the propinquity of a powerful nation whose language and culture have for two hundred years set their stamp upon the civilized world, and whose natural tendency to expansion was as logical as it seemed at times to be dangerous to its neighbors, was at least a problem. It could be a menace, or it could be a protection. It has been both in turn. Having no natural boundaries to the north, the French kings were often tempted to get hold of Flanders, one of the richest territories in Europe, which theoretically belonged to their suzerainty. In this policy they were frustrated and defeated, but in the nineteenth century, when the romantic concept of linguistic nationalism sprang up, a new form of penetration developed. The idea was circulated that a common language, and a common language alone, was the determining factor of nationality, and that all those who spoke a certain idiom belonged in the same nation, regardless of their political allegiance. This attractive and deceptive theory put the individuality of nations to a test. If a nation resisted the physical and cultural attraction which a great country like France could exercise upon it, then there seemed proof enough that it was not only a political but a moral entity as well—a nation. A great number of the Swiss speak French—38 per cent of the Belgians do not know any other tongue—but neither the Swiss nor the Belgians have ever wanted to give up their own character and allegiance or to have their country become a French province.

As Bernard Shaw, referring to the United States and Great Britain, said so well, the French-speaking Swiss and the French-speaking Belgians "are separated [from France] by the same language." This means that, although using the same idiom, although nourished with the same spiritual food, they see no reason why they should join a nation which has undergone experiences, political as well as moral, far different from their own and with which they feel no patriotic solidarity. For seven centuries at least they have had their own life to live, and never have they given up the hope of doing so.

The story of the relations between France and Belgium through the ages would indeed afford a good résumé of European history. There was a time, far back in the Middle Ages, when France's cultural influence upon Belgium was practically nil. In the twelfth and thirteenth centuries the riches and the power of expansion of the Flemish municipalities were such that "to flemish" (to do, to speak, to dress like the Flemings) was a true stamp of elegance and a touchstone of snobbism all over western Europe. At that time even the British feared that the Flemish merchants would gain control of "the narrow sea," the North Sea, and they were literally terrorized at the thought of "the Flemings and their guile." That period was short-lived. Close on the heels of the insolent Flemish cities, France constituted herself on a centralized basis and by her size and wealth in men and material, as well as through her spiritual radiation, became the leading power in Europe.

Oddly enough the most completely Latin part of Bel-

gium has always been within the orbit of Germany, while
the most characteristically Germanic element, Flanders,
has been constantly under the political and intellectual influence of France.

Many times during the fight for the establishment of a
balance of power on the continent, the French came back
to Belgium, either as invaders or as protectors. When
Louis XIV pranced under the walls of Audenarde, Boileau
asked him to stop his victories so that he, Boileau, could
stop writing his odes. Later the French revolutionists got
a poor welcome, chiefly on account of their aggressive
atheism, but the Napoleonic regime was accepted to the
extent that when the King of Rome was born, thirty-one
Flemish poets and only eleven French-writing Belgians
took part in the literary contest organized by an obsequi-
ous *préfet.* But the French administrators wrote in their
reports the significant sentence: "These people are not
Dutchmen; they are certainly not Frenchmen; they are
Belgians."

The French helped and inspired the Belgian revolution
in 1830, and there may have been one or another among
the most exalted of the Belgians who desired an *Anschluss*
with France. But the National Congress was completely
Belgian, and when it had to select a sovereign, it invited a
young prince reared in England. When the Belgian revolution was menaced in 1831, the French generously and
magnanimously intervened and beat off the attack. It is
well known that Napoleon III, in his opaque political
cogitations, contemplated the annexation or the partition
of Belgium, but this fantasy was quite unusual in French
policy and the idea was never part of sound French thinking. It took Darlan to reconsider it, it took the Vichy re-

gime to revive it, in order to compensate for the losses of
territory the Vichyites had agreed upon elsewhere. In 1941
Darlan told a group of officers that France's territorial
losses in the East would be compensated through the annexation of part of Belgium, and an underground Belgian
Walloon newspaper denounced the fact that the Vichy
regime had been paying subsidies to a Belgian separatist
traitor for some unsuccessful propaganda along that line.
It is a clear symptom of an unsound state of affairs in
France when those in power revert to a mistaken idea
which cost the Kings of France many a defeat.

There is, in this world, no better vehicle of sympathy
than the cultural achievements of a nation. The well-
known phrase, "They do those things so well in France,"
is an homage to French character and psychology which is
the result of the prestige of French achievements in the
domain of the intellect and in the realm of art. Such has
been France's influence in Belgium that among the greatest writers whom Belgium produced in the nineteenth century at least two did not speak French as their native
tongue; Maeterlinck and Verhaeren, however, both contributed greatly to French literature, as did Chastellain and
Commines in the fifteenth century.

It has been said and repeated that the Flemings were
opposed to French culture while the Walloons readily accepted it, but nowhere in Europe was a writer like Paul
Claudel as popular as in Flanders. His plays belonged to
the repertoire of all Flemish theaters, and there was no village in Flanders which had not been favored with translations of his *Annonce* or with excellent translations of
Molière's plays. It is possible that the rationalistic trend of
French thinking appealed more to the Walloons than to

the Flemings, but both found in French art and culture inspiration and strength.

These people do not hold France responsible for the ineptitudes uttered by a nervous Reynaud at the end of May, 1940. They know nothing can deprive France of playing a role in Europe—that peace, order and security in Belgium depend to a great extent on a vigorous, strong France. They have faith in this country which twice in a lifetime came to help them and whose sons died on Belgian territory in the common defense of Belgium and France. They believe too that France has an intellectual function in this world. She no longer dominates political thinking, but she can be trusted to think correctly and, when need be, to act with courage and clarity. Inevitably conflicts will arise between Anglo-Saxon and European psychology. In these circumstances it is a safe bet to observe what the true Frenchmen do: most of the time they can be accepted as spokesmen of a free Europe. That thought inspired the Belgian government when it was the first to send a representative to the French Committee in Algiers. That feeling inspires the Belgians and, it may safely be said, will animate most of the European exiles when they see how the French follow a policy of determination and logical thinking which is in the revolutionary tradition of that great country. A people like the French cannot accept anything else; it is against their very nature, against everything they and those nations in Europe which have derived their laws and their philosophical credos from the French stand for.

The example given by the Pucheu trial, regardless of what strictly juridical minds think of it, has borne fruit in Belgium as well as in France. More and more the traitors get jittery, they prepare their retreat, they arrange their files to prove that after having behaved like scoundrels for three years, they had one decent moment. It will be of no avail, as it has been of no avail to Pucheu. Justice will be done. The French killed Darlan, the French executed Pucheu, the French say that in a new Europe they will decide on their own fate and put their own country in order, and the Belgians all over the world, watching this spectacle of moral courage and political integrity, which should be at the basis of every sound national life, approve, and repeat wisely with Dorothy Parker, echoing the earlier sentiments of Sterne,

> They do those things so well in France.

11.—On Bombing German Cities

FOLLOWING THE EXAMPLE OF SOME BRITISH CLERICS, A number of more or less prominent American churchmen have publicly made known their disapproval of the bombing of German cities by Allied airplanes. With no apparent claim to any knowledge of military strategy, they base their attitude on considerations essentially moral.

Anybody who looks at facts from such a standpoint deserves respect and, at the very least, a minimum of attention. Usually those who stand up on such grounds are brave, courageous, forthright people who, regardless of their convictions, are extremely likable. Although in this case they do not aspire to the fate of the martyr (which means properly the *witness*), they put themselves on the threshold of martyrdom because they brave established public opinion. It is well known that, one thing leading to another, they may suffer insult and even injury some day for their belief.

But is it enough to brave public opinion to be right? Unfortunately not. The Doukhobors feel that from time to time, even in sub-zero weather, they have to strip completely and in a group, a practice to which the Canadian constabulary consistently objects. These guardians of the law cannot allow a group of people to walk down the snow-filled streets of Saskatchewan villages, clad only in their birthday suits. But the Doukhobors are brave people, and every time they feel the spirit they repeat their nudist fantasies. Now everybody who knows only a little about the Canadian winter readily understands that the Doukhobors, for all their idealism and bravery, are mistaken.

The founders of the Mormon faith felt that plural marriage was not only a right but a duty of man. Brigham Young had nineteen wives. It is quite certain that lewdness did not incite these people to found such large families. They were probably sincere and honest in their opinions but, according to the experience of most of us, what they undertook can't be done. Apart from all other considerations, only very exceptional men could keep house with one or two dozen women. Very few would dare undertake it. It is evident that these Latter-day Saints were wrong, but from the spiritual standpoint they were respectable idealists and some died as martyrs to their cause.

One is not at all sure of dying for a good cause; one is not at all sure, when speaking out bravely, of saying the right thing. We tell young people to take Polonius' advice, —"To thine own self be true"—but we forget to stress the fact that Polonius was a babbling old fool and by no means a Socrates. Probably only the intentions count and everything will come out right in the end, but in the meantime people who falsify issues or who upset the balance of sentiment and reasoning should be brought back to the real gist of the problem.

If we contend that cities should not be bombed, we imply that there is an essential difference between a soldier and a citizen, between women and men. A civilian, according to this theory, is a sacred being; he should not, he may not die a violent death. The fighting and dying are to be done by the young able-bodied people, but all the older people and all those who for some reason or other are not in the front line, should sit back and relax, looking at the fighting as if it were a football game. They may lose a husband, a son, or a brother, but to themselves no harm whatsoever should be done.

Through the ages it has been the constant effort of the jurists to circumscribe the effects of war. In olden times a vanquished people was torn from its soil, the women becoming the servants and concubines of the victor, the men slaughtered or sold as slaves in foreign lands, property being looted or destroyed. The whole people suffered the fate of the warrior. In the Middle Ages an attempt was made to simplify matters, to reduce international or dynastic troubles to personal conflicts, to transform war into a single man-to-man duel. It sometimes worked. Later on, jurists stepped in and succeeded in persuading nations to accept some kind of understanding to the effect that recruited armies would do all the fighting and that there was an essential difference between a military and a civilian objective. War was due not so much to an uprising of national feeling, it was part of the diplomatic game, it was, as the inscription on Louis XIV's cannon had it: *ultima ratio regis,* the last *argument* of kings, but still an argument. The rest was the affair of strategists, specialists in warfare. They established a front, broke the adversary's line, and the war was over. The results for the vanquished were purely financial and economic. The civilians put up nice monuments to the dead, delivered impressive speeches, and the veterans looked for unobtainable jobs.

It took the Germans to change all that. For over a century they have tended to deify the State—not the people, but the machinery to discipline the people. Once one admits that the greatness of the State is to be the supreme goal of every citizen's life, that reverence for that machinery is not only a duty but a virtue, that the individual does not count but that the State should be an invisible Moloch for which men should live and die, there is but one step to go to reach the road to barbarism, to the conviction that when the nation goes to the attack, nobody should be spared and that, as in Tacitus' time, warriors should be followed by their wives bringing weapons and by their children running errands for their fighting parents. If it is, according to the classics, a wonderful fate to die for the fatherland when one is a soldier, it should be no less an honor for the civilian. Why should the nation be more concerned about the death of an old man than about the sacrifice of an able-bodied youngster? Since men are only "human material," let us not wail about the "waste." Such is the basis of the total-war idea.

If we had good photographs of German women and children killed by Allied air attacks, we should undoubtedly be moved by the gruesome spectacle and nobody would "enjoy" it. Those who have suffered bodily from German brutality or whose parents and dear ones have been tortured by the Gestapo police or have otherwise undergone German ruthlessness, those people—and there are millions of them—would look for a moment at these pictures dry-eyed, and comment, "They got what they asked for and what they deserve." And they would go about their business.

It should always be remembered that this is the first time in a century that the Germans have experienced war on their own territory. The horrors of the procedure were unknown to them. Ruins were something you made elsewhere, they were not to be seen in the Reich. After the war you buried the dead, you kept the wounded off the streets and, since you were beaten, you even turned that to your advantage and inscribed your monuments with that splendid Latin phrase, *Invictis victi victuri*—"To the unbeaten the beaten who will be victorious." But the greatest horror Germany experienced was to have to multiply the figures in marks on the taximeter by 10,000,000—economic disaster. Now the people of Berlin, of Munich, of Hamburg and of Mannheim are learning their lesson. They have always considered a gentlemanly attitude a

of weakness. They want to bully others, not to be
ked on the head themselves. They understand the law
tion, an eye for an eye, a tooth for a tooth, and to
ey understand even better that variation on
the Communists used for some time in
n: "For an eye both eyes and for a tooth
s."

civilians of Germany—and who is a civilian
try?—want the American raids to stop, let
ring up the Swiss or the Swedish ambassador
these gentlemen the news that they have had
of it Everything will be over in twenty-four hours.
won't do it, because they themselves started the prac-
f bombing open cities. That great warrior Badoglio
led ramshackle native Ethiopian villages by that prac-
nd so he became Duke of Addis Ababa. In Guernica
tics were also used successfully. In Rotterdam the
ved effective, and in Tournai, in Nivelles and a
places. The civilians of Ethiopia, of Spain, of
d of Belgium are made of exactly the same flesh
s those of Moabit-Berlin and of Köln-Deutz,
r contests it.

dupes and dopes. Americans should not
vers against Japs, but Japs can go on kill-
d pilots. Hitler can kill 50,000 British civil-
Dutchmen in Rotterdam and 10,000 Belgians
d, but we can't do harm to a German city? We
cause we are human and the enemy is inhuman?
nothing human about war. Its aim is to break the
physically and morally. If the fight can be kept
certain limits, all the better, but that depends on

the fighters. The fighting will always descend to the l
of the meanest of them. That should be allowed in
ness to the gentleman.

Hitler and Mussolini asked for the air
got them. It is regrettable that they did s
great moral advantage besides its militar
the Germans what the word war really mea
gloria, victoria, but women and children blov
houses demolished, darkness, filth and unen
The Germans are hard of hearing. They have ne
the voices of reason and of wisdom. They may lis

When Ulysses went down to Hades he tried to s
the ghosts of the great men and women who
around in the underworld. They could not speak t
until they were given blood to drink. He could not
the eternal truths about destiny and the fate of the
unless they were given this terrible potion.

Of the invisible spirits who lead the world t
people have asked for the third time in a centu
ominous question. At last they are giving bl
spirits to drink. Let us hope that they will u
message. As long as they don't, they will he
the Allied air fleets: a terrible but comfor

12.—*On Daydreams and Democracy*

WE ARE ENTITLED TO OUR DREAMS: TO THOSE WHICH come by night and so smoothly efface the boundaries between reality and fantasy, freeing us from the limitations of the outside world, which are apt in the long run to kill our energies and depress our spirit. We are told that the longest dream lasts only from two to three minutes, but in that short time we can go through a hundred adventures until fear or an overburdening joy awake us. At least when sleeping we live "dangerously." But we also deserve our daydreams. They are a safety valve and a consolation. The tired executive in his office, with the rain streaming down his windowpanes, talks about sunshine and palms. The traveler in his hotel room—it hasn't been "made" yet on account of the personnel shortage—alone with his pipe and a soiled Gideon Bible, longs for his fireplace at home. The intellectual fighting against an unending avalanche of books says, "I'll take to the woods," and the farmer's daughter wants to see Broadway.

Those who have no daydreams or who have given them up, get drunk: on words, on rhythm, on work, on drink. Drinking is the easiest way of shedding the thousand shackles that bind us to our duties, our sorrows and the manifold other forms of our mediocrity. A wise man never blames a drunkard. He almost never blames anybody but himself. Moralists strafe hepcats for their rhythmic orgies and predict the downfall of our civilization if Frank Sinatra is allowed to go on cooing to lovelorn youngsters. Why shouldn't these young people think that the world is just romance and moonshine? Who would have the heart to deprive them of that vigorous and grave exercise they call rug cutting, if that is the only way they have of escaping boredom and a feeling of uselessness which is the greatest menace of youth?

We have our individual dreams, but we also have our dreams in common. We dream as Joe Doakes, but we also dream by contagion, as citizens; we have our national and even our international daydreams. Right now our dream is to see democracy established all over the world. Such is our ideal. Americans know very well that democracy in these United States is far from perfect, that a lot is to be done, and that several groups in this country feel that it is sheer hypocrisy to proclaim a belief in democracy and at the same time permit conditions to exist which are shameful from the human standpoint. They know too that some people associate democracy with lawlessness and they remember the astonishing answer two girls gave when arrested for picking flowers in a public park: "They're ours as well as anybody else's, aren't they? This is a democracy!"

It is inevitable that when dealing with an idea as important and delicate as the democratic faith, misinterpretations will arise. Religion may lead to enraptured mysticism, but ever so often it leads to plain bigotry. Politics can lead to statesmanship, but it can also occasion vulgar graft. Human nature is such that any noble idea suffers from being successively handled by more or less intelligent or interested people. Fortunately public interest among the Allied nations in the democratic idea does not suffer from selfish motives. After all, it matters little to the average American if the Bolivians or the Uruguayans decide to have a Fascist or a democratic form of government. But if these people take the wrong course he will be genuinely affected, because he feels it is a pity that they should err on the road to a better world, his dreamland, his universal Utopia.

With anxiety and even with tenderness, Americans ask the question: "Will Belgium be a democracy after the war?" And they are wont to add: "Will the monarchy go on?" It was Rabelais who first remarked, "Half the world does not know how the other half lives." In Rabelais' time this may have been of little importance, because one hemisphere could not learn anything from the other, but now that the Western hemisphere has found its way, has developed a mode of living and a conception of world relations different from Eurasia, it is imperative that we should know each other better. The United States has applied or tried to apply democracy on a large scale: it has succeeded. In its rightful satisfaction with this remarkable success the United States sometimes forgets that democracy was not invented here, that it has been practiced and has worked effectively for many centuries in several European countries. Bringing democracy to Belgium, for instance, would be carrying coals to Newcastle.

Of course we owe everything to the Greeks; no better, no more eloquent defense of local democracy has ever been given than the one the historian of the Peloponnesian War, Thucydides, records as being delivered by Pericles on the dead of Athens. Pericles does not exalt "Greek" democracy. No, he pictures the political regime of Athens, a small town according to our modern concepts, but in that city the majority rules, there is no compulsion as in Sparta, there are no secret weapons. Any stranger can walk around and observe the defenses of the town. But although nobody is educated for war, in times of danger everybody goes out and fights with determination and valor. Among these "amateurs" in warfare, these "military idiots," as the Spartans esteemed them, the love of the democratic homeland was so great that the tomb of Aeschylus, the father of the Greek drama, is inscribed not with any reference to his tragedies, but with the words, "of his noble prowess the grove of Marathon can speak."

The Belgian cities, especially the towns of Flanders, have for seven centuries studied democracy *in anima vili,* as experimental subjects. The towns originated around a feudal castle or around a prosperous abbey and, when the inhabitants had grown numerous enough they exacted certain concessions from the feudal lords or abbots. They made a contract, they received a charter defining their rights and their obligations. Of course the lord did not wish to lose face in the proceedings. He stuck to the theory that his power was a hereditary and celestial privilege. If he consented to abandon a fragment of his authority, that act should be considered a gracious gesture on his part. He "granted" rights, he did not simply abandon them. The communes developed, they became powerful city republics, they oppressed the smaller townships, they fought each other. Often they attained their autonomy and their independence at the highest cost. Inside their walls, just as Athens did, they achieved democracy. They had to get rid of the patricians who for a while transformed the system into an oligarchy, and very often the common people, in their endeavor for better representation in the city government, were helped by the local rulers. The organized guilds wanted to have their share in the commonwealth: they fought and defeated the patricians. Then opposition arose between the guilds; one group, the weavers, say, or the fullers, wanted to dominate. Bloody encounters followed, but order finally prevailed. Democracy was achieved. It has been Belgium's rule since then. Most of the present-day Belgian villages originated before 1250. In the seven hundred years that separate them from their origin they have always believed in government of the people, by the people, and for the people.

But even those Americans who are familiar with these basic facts of Belgian history seem to feel that a monarchy cannot be a real democracy. In some way they associate monarchy, even constitutional monarchy, with royal despotism, with tyranny—benevolent tyranny, but tyranny still. The revolutionaries who secured Belgium's independence in 1830 and drew up the Belgian constitution, were young men. One of the most influential among them, Nothomb, was only twenty-five years of age. They were extremely liberal in their views, and their discussions resulted in a document which was copied by several other European countries which have come of age since then—Rumania, for instance—and so wise had they been that for more than fifty years no really important change had to be made in this text, notwithstanding the rapid and radical changes in the social and economic aspect of the kingdom. The authors of the Belgian constitution did not want the king to be a despot. In fact, they gave him very little real power. They stated as a principle that "all power comes from the nation." The king is supposed to be the arbiter above the parties, the umpire among the political tendencies. He is bound by his oath to the constitution. It is said very clearly that he is the king "of the Belgians" not "of Belgium," that he is a symbol of national unity and not the proprietor of the country. He does not own Belgium, the country owns him.

The only party ever to proclaim the republican principle in Belgium has long since dropped this argument and there has never been any instance of one of the kings of the Belgians trying to slow down the democratic evolution of the country. Universal suffrage was achieved after the last war, following a royal promise in 1918.

The Americas had to fight kings and emperors to secure their freedom. In Europe most of the countries settled the relation between king and people once for all a long time ago. People there know that there is nothing incompatible between a democratic regime and the existence of a monarch. Confusion arises when those terms are used in an archaic sense. Confucius, the very enemy of confusion (excuse the moronic pun), once said:

"A superior man considers it necessary that the names he uses be spoken appropriately. What the superior man requires is just that in his words there may be nothing incorrect."

Would it be too daring a daydream to hope that when this war is over the word democracy will be understood everywhere correctly, so that "the superior man" may be happy, with a solid chance for the not-so-superior individual to share in this intellectual and political bonanza?

13.—Should We "Lay That Pistol Down"?

IT IS SAID IN PROVERBS (XXVII, 22) THAT, "THOUGH thou shouldest bray a fool in a mortar among wheat with a pestle, yet will not his foolishness depart from him." In fact, this Biblical pronouncement is an understatement. When we consider that ten months after Pearl Harbor a university professor was afraid that after the war there might not be "a secure Japan," that now when Allied victory is assured in Europe some people here organize a movement for "Peace Now," including in their program a desire for "kindness" toward Germany and Japan—when we consider that and many other manifestations of universally disordered reasoning—there is sufficient evidence to suppose that Solomon in his proverb did not indulge in oriental exaggeration.

In a world of drama fools are a necessity, but they must be at least amusing, or else purely lyrical, like that charming character in *As You Like It,* "who laid him down and bask'd him in the sun." But pedantic or idealistic fools are a plague.

At the end of the fifteenth and the beginning of the sixteenth centuries the best literature dealt with the endless variety of foolishness as it was displayed in the world at that time. The two outstanding books, Sebastian Brandt's *Ship of Fools* and Erasmus' *In Praise of Folly,* did not exhaust the theme, for minor moralists of all nations tried during the seventeenth century to catalogue in the most detailed manner the thousand different ways in which man is capable of manifesting his lack of balance.

It is quite certain—and to some extent reassuring—that we all participate in some folly or other, and that a given time and specific events are needed to make us understand where we erred or deviated from the safe but unattractive path of reason. This war has helped many of us to see our past follies and mistakes. It has, however, proved a rather paradoxical point, namely, that the very man we rightly consider the paranoiac chief of the German people is the only one who fifteen years ago wrote down what he intended to do and with iron logic set himself to do it! Hitler has made a full feature film out of *Mein Kampf.* His folly lies in the absolutism of his views, but the major part of his policy was inspired by a clear purpose, which he pursued without faltering. His folly was essentially the folly of grandeur.

The spectacle of human lunacy is far more entrancing and colorful on the Allied side of the world. That follies such as the ones cited above are possible during this war is not astonishing when we look at the way we behaved only a few years before the war broke out. Let us leave the statesmen alone; some of them proved their ignorance, some were guilty of criminal negligence and stupidity, some were far-sighted and courageous.

It is useless to blame them individually, because each one of them reflected a trend of public opinion. One of the dangers of a democratic state is the temptation for a representative of the nation, be he a member of parliament or a minister, to consider himself as just the mouthpiece of his constituents and to abandon any desire of guiding them, of helping them form their opinions with the benefit of the wider knowledge and information he himself has acquired.

To be a politician is to specialize, to study how to bring about the general good, to document oneself as completely as possible, and to consider public affairs on that basis, while public sentiment as a rule merely follows its emotional inclination. Most of the time the unpopular statesmen prove to be right in the end, but all too few of them find the courage to brave unpopularity. They prefer to be accomplices of the weaknesses and follies of their countrymen.

It is therefore highly instructive to look back at some highlights of the prewar period as recorded in the frank confessions of those who tell of their mistakes. Certainly one of the most candid and enlightening accounts is by that clever and witty author, Beverley Nichols. In *Men Do Not Weep* * he tells us some surprising things about the state of mind of some people in Europe only a few years before the war.

Mr. Beverley Nichols was a pacifist, which would have been perfectly all right if he had tried to apply his theories only to his native land. But one day he heard that a

* New York, Harcourt, Brace, 1942, pp. 100-102.

few young people in Belgium had refused to serve in the
army, partly on internal political grounds, partly because
of pacifist arguments. He thought: "If only those young
men had had their way . . . if only the world had listened
to them." He left posthaste for Brussels to get in touch
with these heroes. Their lawyer would help him. This man
proved to be quite a disappointment. His office "was just
the sort of office a pacifist ought *not* to have," and the
man himself "was just the sort of man a pacifist ought *not*
to be. Small, pale, shrill-voiced, nervous." He arranged for
Mr. Nichols to see the pacifists, who were in prison. But
Mr. Nichols never got in touch with them, for he was received by a Belgian officer, and a most enlightening conversation developed. His account of the interview follows:

An officer was standing in the doorway. He was very tall, and
everything about him was narrow, his face, his eyes, his lips, his
shoulders . . . and, as I was soon to find, his mind.

"You were waiting to see Monsieur le Commandant?"

"If you please."

He closed the door. "Your papers, please."

He studied them carefully, and handed them back. Then he
said:

"Why do you wish to see these men, monsieur?"

"To bring them some little consolation."

"To encourage them in their obstinacy?"

"I would not put it like that."

"Then how would you put it?"

"I would prefer to discuss that with the Commandant."

"I regret that you must first discuss it with me."

We were not liking each other very much, but nothing would
be gained by losing my temper, so I said:

"I do not regard these men as criminals, monsieur. I regard
them as pioneers."

"So that you would like all Belgians to follow their example?"

"Not only all Belgians, but all the world."

"We are not talking about all the world. We are talking about Belgium. You would like to see all Belgians follow their example?"

I saw the trap opening. (It is so tragically easy to lay traps for pacifists.) I tried to avoid it.

"That is hardly probable, is it, monsieur?"

"We are not talking about probabilities," he snapped. "We are talking about your aims. For the third time, you would like to see all Belgians follow their example?"

The trap was drawing tighter. I chose my words carefully. "I think that such an event might mark a new era in the history of civilization."

"Then your answer is 'yes'?"

"Yes."

His lips tightened. He reached out his hand for my papers. First the passport, then the letter from J . . ., then the special police permit. He handed them over one by one, in silence. Then he said, "I regret, monsieur . . ." He did not finish the sentence, but rose to his feet.

"But . . . my interview? And Monsieur le Commandant?"

He shrugged his shoulders. "I fear that Monsieur le Commandant is too occupied to listen to arguments such as yours."

I stared at him, feeling futile and baffled. Only a few yards away men were being tortured for the cause to which I had hoped to dedicate my life. And this man stood in the way. I tried to fight for time.

"But, monsieur, you have not heard my arguments. . . ."

"On the contrary, I have heard them all too often. And each time with less enjoyment."

He opened the door and stood there waiting. I went out.

The next day Mr. Nichols tried to see the King of the Belgians. "Well, I marched into the palace all right. And within five minutes marched out again." Very discouraged, he walked around, "trying to find some peaceful place in which to sit down, and think clearly."

It is a pity that Mr. Nichols did not try to "think clearly" before acting, which, according to the advice of all sages, is the right thing to do. No, he did not stop at anything. Meddling in the affairs of a foreign country, he came to tell the Belgians how to behave. Only a couple of years before the second invasion of Europe his message to a small, permanently endangered nation was to lay down its arms. "Lay that pistol down!" The Belgian official was "narrow" because, with icy politeness, he wished to impress upon Mr. Nichols that the safety and security of Belgium depended on the willingness of its inhabitants to fight for that security and safety, and that furthermore it was none of Mr. Nichols' concern to tell the Belgians what to do.

It would be unfair to underline the fantastic character of this international episode, now that Mr. Nichols so candidly tells it, but for the distressing fact that in 1943 this author, who must be typical of a class of people in his country, has not a word of self-criticism, that he does not in the least seem to suspect that the Belgians who refused to tolerate conscientious objectors in such a critical period had a clear notion of what was lying ahead for Europe. On the contrary, Mr. Nichols finds it appropriate to ridicule those people who in 1940 held off the German invasion for eighteen days. He persists, and we all know that since the Middle Ages *persevare diabolicum*—to err is human, to persist in one's error is of the devil.

14.—*The Label on the Mustard Pot*

LET US SUPPOSE THAT ALL OF A SUDDEN, OUT OF THE blue sky, the rumor goes about town that Eudora Smith is engaged, betrothed, affianced (or whatever else you have in the repetitious or circumlocutory vocabulary of the society page) to a Mr. Jones. This news item is generally considered a compliment to Eudora, for in our present state of civilization, even in so aggressive a matriarchate as the United States, a young lady is supposed to wait till a Mr. Jones shows sufficient interest in her personality to prefer her company—headaches and toothaches included —to that of any other female.

Let us suppose, however, that the rumor is incorrect. The only thing for Eudora to do is to deny this falsehood and say: "No, no. Mr. Jones is a nice boy, a charming gentleman, a distinguished citizen of the community, but we are not engaged, betrothed, etc., etc."

The more Eudora explains and denies, the more inevitably will her reputation suffer in the proceeding. Her friends will ask each other whether Eudora may have been hasty in letting people suppose that she was engaged or whether Mr. Jones, having found some repulsive fault in Eudora, has retreated from the marital battle line. Poor

Eudora, she'll never be quite the same after this unfortunate incident!

Something of that kind happened to Belgium. It calls for an explanation.

It will be remembered that at the most dramatic moment of the tragedy of France, Churchill threw the doors of the British Commonwealth wide open to all Frenchmen. They did not accept the invitation.

Later, General Jan Smuts, the South African Premier, expressed the wish that, after the war, countries like France, Belgium and Holland would join the British Empire.

Then bold headlines in the American newspapers proclaimed that the Belgian Minister of Information, Mr. Antoine Delfosse, had definitely expressed Belgium's willingness to abandon her sovereign rights and to join the British Commonwealth of Nations.

In a caustic mood the French poet Villiers de l'Isle-Adam once wrote: "There are not thirty people in the whole world really able to read a text, be it even a label on a mustard pot." The veracity of this sad pronouncement was proved by the reactions which the alleged statement of Minister Delfosse provoked.

A great number of people read only the headlines and neglected to read the text of Mr. Delfosse's speech. They shouted, "Bravo! Bravissimo! Europe is finally getting organized; a small nation sacrificing its independence joins a big outfit and simplifies the problem!" Already they had visions of easy traffic through western Europe without vaudevillian customs officers and inspectors interrupting the traveler's slumber every two or three hours to inquire about passports and smuggled cigars.

But, on the other hand, a number of people were upset and scandalized by this "news." They felt that Belgium "would lose most of its charm, having to adopt a new language and all." They could not very well see how the announcement could be true, since the Belgians "are supposed to be exceedingly patriotic."

All these contradictory reactions prove that it was worth while raising the issue. No milk is spilled yet, and before anything happens there is time to clear up whatever misunderstandings have arisen and to state clearly the terms of the debate.

What are these sovereign rights the Belgians are supposed to be willing to abandon? With regard to other nations the sovereignty of a state expresses itself most clearly through an independent foreign policy. A state has supreme authority if it is at liberty to decide in peace as well as in war what side it will take. To be able to do so the state needs an army, armament factories, fortifications, as well as an internal military and civilian organization which makes it as independent as possible of other countries. Of course its geographical position or its lack of essential war materials—and now practically everything has become war material—can deprive it completely of every possibility of real sovereignty. Even then, in order to avoid injuring national pride and for the sake of international good manners, the complete independence of some states is recognized as a matter of course, although it may be merely political window dressing.

Can one abandon *part* of one's sovereign rights? It seems a contradiction in terms. To say that a state will give up *part* of its sovereignty calls to mind the father who was extremely anxious to marry his daughter to a reluctant young man and who whispered reassuringly to the unwilling suitor that the girl was "only a little bit" pregnant. You either give up your sovereignty or you don't. You are either completely master of your political destiny or you're bound for better or for worse to another power which tells you how to behave.

But every treaty, every arrangement one country makes with another limits its freedom of action. Freely made conventions and agreements which contain mutual obligations, however broad their scope, do not diminish the sovereign position of those interested.

It is self-evident that the Belgians, after this war, as after the previous war, will express in political terms their distaste for Germany and their sympathy for those who have delivered them from the Germans. Not only will the Belgian population be ready to collaborate with the Anglo-Saxon democracies in world reconstruction, but they will be eager to find ways to assure a lasting peace in Europe.

It may sometimes sound like a hasty generalization when we say that a whole country likes or dislikes another country, but for Belgium the case is simple: 8,360,000 Belgians have the same reasons to mistrust and even to hate the Germans. They have a sovereign right to express their feelings in their politics; being inhabitants of a small country which, relying solely on its own forces, could not resist Germany, they also have the right to look for protection and help to those who are in a position to defend them. The trend of Belgium's policy after the war is already obvious.

A big country can as a final contingency gamble with its destiny; Germany already has done so twice, because it knows definitely that whatever happens, through its mere bulk, its size, it will subsist among the nations. Nobody is going to *absorb* it. It may conceivably be diminished, amputated, or temporarily dismembered, but it will continue to exist as a nation because it is a bulky mass among smaller entities. We sing in hymns and songs of the crumbling of *empires*. They do indeed crumble when they contain heterogeneous elements, but there is little likelihood that a linguistically homogeneous Germany will fall apart.

A small country must not and should not gamble with its future. It has certain spiritual values to defend, something incalculable and intangible, like the bouquet of an old wine—its personality. Belgium knows by now that there is a permanent menace on its left flank, a constant danger of absorption by Germany. It looks for security. Where will it find that security in Europe at this time? In a combination of the small democracies? The idea is tempting and eminently sympathetic, but from the military standpoint impracticable and ineffective. The collective forces of the Netherlands, Belgium, Denmark and Norway cannot possibly stop eighty million Germans.

Will Belgium find security in France? General Smuts pronounced a rather hasty funeral oration on France. Most of the comments on that gloomy utterance stressed the point that France must and will again become a great power in Europe. As neighbors of France the Belgians know her greatness and her weaknesses. Experienced in political ups and downs, they also know that it is not enough to wish to be a great power in order to become one. After all, it was the very first French economist, Jean Bodin, who said: *"Il n'est richesse ni force que d'hommes"*— There is no richness or strength but in men.

To disregard France on the future map of Europe, as General Smuts seemed to do, is to make a reckless prophecy. The spiritual resources of this great country have proven many times that the predictions of her enemies and even of her friends were mistakes. But at the moment the Belgians do not know how strong or how weak France really is: they fervently hope, however, that France will recover from Hitler's blows and from her own internal division. That may take some time. They realize also to what extent Hitler's master plan for the undermining of France's manpower has succeeded: whatever France's position in Europe will be, it is clear that she cannot carry alone the burden of keeping Germany in check.

If therefore the small countries want to rely on Great Britain or the United States, which, traditionally, have protected their existence, which never have shown any territorial ambition toward these countries, nobody should be either astonished or scandalized. If at any time after the war either Belgium or Holland wishes to make a treaty of close co-operation with Great Britain, it is evident that this will not be done by either of them jumping right into the lap of the British Empire. It will be done by "free covenants freely arrived at," which presupposes sacrifices and obligations on *both* sides.

No government in exile in London is in a position to decide now on such important matters. Even if all the Belgians were agreeable to such a capital move, a democratic government would not take such a responsibility when physically separated from its constituents. It is clear that Mr. Delfosse's speech did not carry the implications which have been read into it. In fact, he said: "After this war we intend to maintain the good relations we have always had with Britain. Our interests link us in the same way as our hearts. It is necessary that a big power should take a step to insure peace in Europe. No one could do it better than the British Commonwealth, which has succeeded in gaining the friendship of most people living under the shadow of its flag. It can become a leader of nations, especially in western Europe. We ask but one thing: to be free in our internal regime and to earn our living properly and honestly. We are sure Britain is able to understand us and to give us the fair guaranty we need for our social reconstruction and for the happiness of our people."

So after all Eudora Smith is not engaged, betrothed, etc., but will her reputation suffer from this misunderstanding? It would be unjust and cruel.

III
SOME BELGIAN
PEOPLE

1.—The Average Belgian

Who is the average Belgian? As the farmer who looked at the kangaroo said: "There ain't no such animal." The average Belgian is as nonexistent as the man who corresponds one hundred per cent to the description of Joe Doakes. But on July 21, the Belgian national holiday, every Belgian looks around, likes what he sees, and recognizes his fellow countrymen as such and, not unlike the Lord on the seventh day of creation, approves of what he surveys. For he has, through a kaleidoscopic vision of his fellow countrymen, discovered that mythical creature, the average Belgian.

Before the war the elegant newspapers used to call him, in English and between quotation marks, "the man in the street," and to credit him with a startling array of virtues, leaving him only those few little defects which don't hurt anybody and which rather endear people to us. To be an Englishman, a Belgian or an American is not merely a matter of an official quill driver's record, or a geographical accident. It is partly an unconscious, partly a conscious procedure. One has to will it to a certain extent, to superimpose on all the things that have shaped one's heart and brains a volition to be what most people around one are. That will, like members of other nationalities, the Belgians express on their national holiday, not so much by songs and parades as by a silent agreement that there are a number of things, imponderables, that bind them together, and that those elements which oppose them to each other exist just to keep the system in good working order.

The average Belgian is called van Brabant, van Leemput, van Swinderen, van Steenput, or anything else in "van." This particle does not denote a weakness for nobility, for the Belgian has long since disposed of the anachronistic conception that any man, by putting "van" or "de" before his name, should be allowed to consider himself any better than another man. The "van" denotes nothing else but his place of origin. He is Joseph van Ghent, as Joe Doakes would be Joe from Kankakee, or from Chattahoochee. If he is a Walloon, then he will be Joseph Depuis or Dufour or Delmaison, and the "du" or the "del" would not mean anything more than the "van" of his Flemish counterpart.

This Mr. Josef van So-and-so or Joseph du Such-and-such is the average Belgian. He therefore lives in Brussels, which is a linguistic no man's land, where he may either pretend to understand only one language or contrive to make a mixture of both idioms, the result of which would baffle even those versatile geniuses who invent the formulas for American salads.

The average Belgian is an official, or else his son or uncle is and, if he himself is not, he wants to become one. Not that there is money in it, or that it is a great honor to be in government service, but it stands for security, and unless you kill your wife or run away with the stamps at the office, you stay an official for the rest of your life. The

official's life is mediocre; he is, according to the traditional expression, only a small cog in a big machine, but
he trusts that the machine will go on and permit him to
live an approximately decent life and to have a dignified
funeral.

Or he is a small businessman. The Germans, who still
have time to spare for statistics, recently found out that
there were no fewer than 434,094 commercial enterprises
in Belgium, which means one for every 19 inhabitants of
the country. They discovered also that for every 57 Belgians there is a food-supply establishment. This small businessman—he is a grocer, a baker, a butcher or a confec-
tioner—does not like big business. He hates department
stores because he fears them, and the very idea of a chain
store throws him into a tantrum, for he knows that his
profession is overcrowded and that danger lurks around
every corner.

The big businessman is boastful; the small businessman, like the farmer, does not dare to provoke the fickle
god of trade, Mercury, who postures on every lamppost
of Fifth Avenue. He complains a lot. His lament is not
very lyrical; it is a vague rumbling in the background, the
noise of an anonymous crowd. The middle class, to which
the vast majority of the Belgians belong, is like the choir
in a Greek tragedy, complaining but wise, articulate but
never violent, a safety valve for the nation's temper.

This man has two main topics of conversation, or rather
of recrimination—the weather and the government. Little can be done about the weather, except making fun of
the Royal Meteorological Institute, which always plays
safe and predicts "local showers" every day of the year,
without ever indicating the locality. But you *can* change

the government. He is all for that. His idea is "as little government as possible." He brings to mind those Irishmen, shipwrecked on an island, who met some of the native cannibals and asked, "Is there a government on this island?" When the natives replied that there was, the Irishmen said, "We're against it." Mr. van So-and-so is the same kind. Does that imply that he is a revolutionary? Certainly not. He considers revolution bad taste and is ready to leave that practice to the Argentinians. But he likes to vote any time, and the percentage of Belgians who would rather pay the small fine imposed for not voting is negligible.

He is a liberal. Long before social legislation gave adequate protection to the workers in the United States or in France, he had managed to send to Parliament a majority of members who voted a system of social laws which are considered a model for all Europe: he remembers with shame and horror the days, more than fifty years ago, when strikes were broken with bayonets, and he is impatient at the power some big concerns still retain in the state.

Is the average Belgian a religious man? Since the great majority of the Belgians are Catholic, the average Belgian belongs to that faith, or at least he lives in a Catholic atmosphere: he is permeated with Catholic ideas. The problem of whether he belongs to the church or not is put to him in a far more definite form than it would be in America. It is indeed not sufficient for him to declare that he is a Christian and that he believes in God in order to comply with public opinion, for if he does so he is supposed to be a regular church member and to take an active part in the life of his religious community. He will be either a devout Catholic or an active unbeliever, but being fond of compromise, even if he is the latter he will have his children baptized, his daughter will marry in church, and he will submit to the solemn liturgy of the church when he dies. In politics, however, he will be violently anticlerical, leaving religion "to the women." He will look with irony and compassion at those few aggressive anticlericals who ostentatiously eat steak on Friday, and his attitude toward metaphysics will be strongly influenced by a popular adaptation of the famous wager of Pascal, according to which those who are not quite certain of life after death have nothing to lose by believing in it.

All of us secretly long for the day when we shall have nothing more to do, when we shall be delivered from office work, teaching, or any other occupation and when we shall be able to free ourselves from the violent encroachments on our privacy made by the telephone, so well depicted as a horrible menace by Salvador Dali. What will we do then, when we have nothing to do? The answer should show very clearly our real nature. What do the Belgians do when they have nothing to do? Most of the time they enjoy their family life, or they go and sit in their cafés, of which there are about one to every ten persons.

There, among the soothing noises of conversations, of the beer glasses knocking on the tables, the cash register ringing constantly, the few exclamations of card players, the sound of dice softly rolling on the green cloth or the dry shock of the billiard balls, the average Belgian meditates, puffs his pipe or talks to his lifelong friends. After twenty years the Belgian who has made his fortune in the United States, who has become one hundred and fifty per cent American, who loves this country dearly, will sigh deeply and say, "There are no cafés in America; that is really a pity." The Greeks sought wisdom under the porticoes of Athens, endlessly discussing public affairs and eternal truths; the Belgians make every café into an antechamber of Parliament, into an abode of everyday wisdom. Women go to cafés too, but by the orthodox café visitors they are considered intruders, and a woman who ventures to visit a café regularly is criticized for it: one should leave the quest of truth to the men.

Joseph van So-and-so is a kind man. He may not have the exaggerated sentimentality with regard to animals which causes him to be so amazed when he observes the English, but he likes his fellow men and is charitable to them. He likes gossip because he has an intense interest in everything human, and at heart he is romantic. The wild gestures of passion appeal to him because they contain a lesson, and he is not overproud to have mastered the seven demons which inhabit every one of us, for he has read in the Scriptures that if you chase out those seven, seventy-seven come back to attack and destroy you. Truly, he is a wise and well-balanced man.

If you ask him of what he is the most proud, what is his greatest quality, he will not say: I am a great painter, I am a great poet, I invent new ways to master the elements, I am a great fighter, although he could quote the names of many a great painter, many a great poet, many a great man of enterprise and technical ingenuity. No, he will be at the same time modest and extremely proud. He will answer: My main quality is common sense! Genius does not like common sense and is apt to consider it a proof of bourgeois baseness, of down-to-earth tendencies, but it is a quality so rare among men, so seldom encountered on a nation-wide scale that the Belgian is conscious of this exception.

That common sense tells the average Belgian that no man is better than another, that tyranny is vile and that when the hour comes to fight for liberty one has to do it and do it well. He is neither heroic in his features nor in his language. He is a plain blunt man who likes to live in peace, but he fights "like a lion" when the hour of danger arrives. He could say:

"Our constitution does not copy the laws of neighboring states; we are rather a pattern to others than imitators ourselves. Its administration favors the many instead of the few; this is why it is called a democracy. If we look to the laws, they afford equal justice to all in their private differences; as to social standing, advancement in public life falls to reputation for capacity, class consideration not being allowed to interfere with merit, nor again does poverty bar the way. If a man is able to serve the state, he is not hindered by the obscurity of his condition. The freedom which we enjoy in our government extends also to our ordinary life. There, far from exercising a jealous surveillance over each other, we do not feel called upon to be angry with our neighbor for doing what he likes, or even to indulge in those injurious looks which cannot fail to be offensive, although they inflict no positive penalty. But all this ease in our private relations does not make us lawless as citizens."

This he could say, adapting the immortal words Thucydides puts into the mouth of Pericles when praising Athens. He would not be presumptuous in so doing, for he has shown the world for many a century that gesturing is not heroism and that there is greatness in simplicity.

If therefore on July 21 he looks around and "sees everything that he has made" and finds it is "very good," do not blame him for that moment of national pride: he is perfectly entitled to that weakness in which many others indulge the year round.

2.—"Modern Medicine Begins Here"

At times, war seems to be as hard on some dead people as it is on the living. Look at what happened, for instance, to a gentleman from Brussels, one Andreas van Wezel, born in 1514. When everybody all over the world was set and ready to celebrate the four hundredth anniversary of his birth, Kaiser Wilhelm, the great promoter of fresh and invigorating warfare, was taking up all the space in the newspapers and celebrations had to be postponed indefinitely.

In 1943, a number of scholarly individuals wanted to draw the attention of the world to the fact that four hundred years ago the same Mr. van Wezel had published a most remarkable book. Immediately a buffoon of the first magnitude, one Benito Mussolini, succeeded in diverting the world's attention from all academic pursuits. Therefore, it seems right and just that, abandoning present-day history for once and turning from our Belgian wailing wall, we go back into Belgium's past to do justice to a man who, according to those who know, was a real benefactor of mankind.

To a certain extent, all of us are interested in anatomy, but most people—caring only about the pleasant side of it —stop at the surface and disregard what is going on inside. This should not provoke our astonishment or our indignation. How many millions of people drive a car who know nothing and care even less about what makes the thing go. Taking a reasonable and sound attitude toward a mechanical contraption which should serve us and not dominate our lives, they become interested only when it stops. But, of course, people who are supposed to keep the human anatomy going, as well as those who have to repair cars, must be informed about the contents of the mechanism they tend.

It is really a miracle of human negligence that not before 1543 did anybody really care to find out or have the courage to investigate how the human body was "fabricated." In the beginning of our era, the Greek scholar Galen made some clever deductions on human anatomy from his observations of animal life, but it took Mr. van Wezel, who called himself in Latin Vesalius, to liberate humanity from an ignorance that was all the more astonishing as the means to do away with it were so easy. In 1543 he published, in Basel, what is perhaps the greatest achievement of Belgian science, his book on the construction of the human body: *De Humani Corporis Fabrica*. It is considered as ranking among such works as Copernicus' book on the *Revolution of the Spheres,* Adam Smith's *Wealth of Nations* and Darwin's *Origin of Species.* It has been said by authoritative men that with Vesalius' book "modern medicine begins." It has also been said that his great work is "one of the most nobly illustrated volumes in the world."

Vesalius had to fight the prejudices of the Church as well as those of the medical profession—no small undertaking. To some Church people his work looked like desecration. To the medical faculty, he seemed a troublesome, revolutionary spirit who dared to doubt the authority of the scientific demigod Galen. It must be said that his methods of investigation were bound to arouse suspicion. He specialized in taking the bodies of executed criminals from the gibbets and the gallows. In Louvain he had a real field day when he took home the body of a noted robber who, "since he deserved more than ordinary hanging, had been chained to the top of a high stake and roasted alive over a slow fire made of straw, kept burning some distance below his feet. In this way a dish had been cooked for the fowls of the air, which they regarded as a special dainty. The bones, therefore, had been elaborately picked, and there was left suspended on the stake a skeleton dissected and cleaned with rare precision by many beaks. The dazzling skeleton, neat and polished, was lifted on high. . . ."

It was a proof of the fine and independent spirit of Emperor Charles V that he chose this man as his house physician and it was rather astonishing that his son, Philip II, a retrograde and a bigot if there ever was one, kept Vesalius in his service after the death of the Emperor. Vesalius was sometimes in great need of official protection, and toward the end of his life he barely escaped a cruel death. The legend says that he had made a study of the corpse of a young Spanish nobleman. The combined efforts of the gentlemen of the Inquisition, of the members of the Faculty of Medicine and of the young man's relatives were to prove that the object of Vesalius' anatomical carvings was not completely dead when the great physician was already dissecting his nerves and bones. These three groups of people feared that, especially in this case, haste was of the devil.

Reaction was so strong that Vesalius, although getting away with his life, had to go on a pilgrimage to Jerusalem to expiate his sin of inquisitiveness. He died on his way home on the island of Zante, which Homer so lovingly called "wood-shaded Zakynthos."

Vesalius' work on the human body was published when he was twenty-eight years of age. Apart from a theoretic exposé, it contained a great number of beautiful engravings representing the human body and skeleton in different states and attitudes. These remarkable engravings were made by a Flemish artist, Jan van Calcar, a talented pupil of Titian. The skeletons and otherwise dissected humans do not stand at attention as they do in our modern encyclopaedias, looking horribly bored and impersonal. They strike all kinds of attitudes expressing sorrow, dignity, deep thinking, etc. One of them has a long knife in one hand, while with the other he holds aloft his entire skin of which he has apparently divested himself in the interest of science.

The American Medical Library Association has printed a bulletin entirely dedicated to Vesalius' great work. Connoisseurs have pointed out that the Calcar engravings may be considered "stylistic forerunners of Surrealism" and that the anatomies of Vesalius find their counterpart in some fantasies by modern painters like George de Chirico and Salvador Dali.

These artistic comments are of course very flattering, but they scarcely do justice to the Belgian scientist, and they divert attention from the fact that Vesalius is only a link in the impressive chain of Belgian scholars who have contributed, down through the ages, to the advancement of medicine and surgery. Before Vesalius, there was Jan Yperman (1294–1357), who wrote a masterly treatise on surgery. A contemporary of Vesalius, Dodonaeus, greatly contributed to the development of pathological anatomy, and his studies on plants and herbs are still of basic importance. Dr. Palfijn (1721) invented the forceps, and in the field of physiology Dr. Theodore Schwann discovered the animal cell. This discovery was called "probably the most important generalization of biology." In modern times, Professor Bordet's creative contributions to bacteriology earned him the Nobel Prize.

By honoring Andreas van Wezel as a Belgian scientist, therefore, the world pays tribute to a long line of scientific men who have greatly advanced human knowledge and who have, to a certain extent at least, made this world what it is.

Somewhere in the Talmud (and don't ask me where, please) it is said that one should be grateful to anyone from whom one learns a sentence, a word or even a letter. It is a good thing that at least in the free world today people express their admiration and their gratitude to that Belgian scientist who, four hundred years ago, found a little truth we were missing, and who, although people called him "an impious madman whose breath poisoned Europe," went about his business of telling us about our

sinews and bones as composedly and at ease as Walt
Whitman when he sang "The Body Electric" and its:

Strong shoulders, manly beard, scapula, hind-shoulders, and the
    ample side-round of the chest,
Upper-arm, armpit, elbow-socket, lower-arm, arm-sinews, arm-
    bones,
Wrist and wrist-joints, hand, palm, knuckles, thumb, forefinger,
    finger-joints, finger-nails. . . .

3.—"I Adorn the World, but I Despise It"

SOME TIME AGO A YOUNG AMERICAN, WHO FOR SOME
reason or other was unable to join the army, was heard
complaining about the fact that for the duration at least
he couldn't see anything of the world. He said in dead
earnest, "I am practically encaged in these United States."

Oh, wonderful cage, and how jealous would be those
millions of people in Europe and elsewhere who all their
lives for religious, political, linguistic, or simply economic
reasons are unable to move farther than one hundred
miles from their homes! But after all, Mr. Paul Morand
wrote a book called *Rien Que La Terre,* a title which
throws the regrets of the young American into the shade.
"Nothing but the earth," says Mr. Morand, and the globe's

dimensions continue to become smaller and narrower while our desires and ambitions are supposed to exceed its size and shape.

The trouble with the world is that we identify ourselves with what we know. To keep our interest in life going we need mystery and excitement—excitement arising out of mystery. We have come to know this old world too well. There are scarcely even a few corners left of which we do not have good maps and surveys. Every school child is familiar with the shape of the earth. Everybody knows that except for a few retreats in the woods along the Amazon, the world will soon look like a model village in a nineteenth-century World's Fair. A few years ago when a certain daring writer and explorer wanted to partake of a genuine two-course cannibal meal, the poor alleged cannibals, although they did not want to offend him, were extremely embarrassed and were forced to serve him a piece of mutton instead. When the movie potentates want to show us a 100 per cent savage, they serve us the impressive anatomy of Johnny Weismuller, who is so highly civilized that he writes books about the art of swimming. No, there is little "nature" left for amateurs. We have to make it up ourselves.

The Golden Age of the dreamers, nature lovers and globe trotters was between 1400 and 1600. Christopher Columbus, as the locker-room song has it, "that navigatin', calculatin', son-of-a-gun, Colombo," unleashed something in millions of minds and hearts from which we all still suffer. When Lindbergh crossed the Atlantic everyone was elated: we—all of us humans—had done something the elements didn't want us to do. It was glorious, but at the same time we felt the earth was shrinking. In our subconscious we understood that in our quest for the truth we would soon no longer have the excuse of going places to find out what other people have discovered. We saw that the solution for our problems was no longer to be found in the study of a diversified mankind but in ourselves. Now there is no place on earth which you can't reach in sixty hours. The fact that mappemondes do not look global any more but have acquired the shape of a trigonometrist's nightmare is but a diversion. The modern man is told that the world is a small, third-rate planet and that we know all about it.

All that started when Ptolemaeus, the Greek, began making maps. Up to 1462 they were still considered worthy of publication, but real map-making and publishing developed only in the sixteenth century. It had nothing to do with any philosophical preoccupation; it was just the answer to a need of the time.

Antwerp, the "gathering place of merchants of all nations," was at that time the economic center of Western Europe. Poets lauded it in exalted rhymes, foreign writers and distinguished visitors praised it as the greatest and richest of all European cities. As an illustration of the theory that art and science need the background of a capitalistic society, one could not find any better example. The rich merchants and financiers not only wanted to be entertained by the artists, they not only asked the painters to represent them and their ponderous spouses on canvas, but they also expected the scientists to make life easier for them by their discoveries or by cataloguing the rudiments of scientific knowledge already existing in certain realms of human endeavor. Like the eighteenth century, the sixteenth is a period not so much of great creative activity as it is one of inventories and encyclopedic surveys.

One of the most urgent requirements of the international crowd that convened in the Antwerp Exchange, the first one to be established in the world, was the need of good maps of Europe, Africa and Asia. Travel was still a hazardous enterprise, distances were poorly defined, errors were manifold in the existing land and coast maps. A whole school of map makers and engravers sprang up, the most famous of all being Mercator, whose projection of the globe has only recently been discarded for a more modern conception. They drew maps, they bought maps from the Italians, the Spaniards and the Portuguese. They redrew and reprinted them and sold them.

Among these sellers of maps was one Abraham Ortelius, born in Antwerp in 1527. He had latinized his inelegant name of Wortel (root) or Ortel into a scholarly-sounding version. By trade he was a merchant. He saw a great deal of Europe and used to go twice a year from his home town to the fairs of Frankfort, a voyage comparable to a transcontinental trip nowadays. He was registered in the artists' union as an *"afzetter van kaarten,"* a vendor of maps.

We know little about his character, but still enough to appreciate him as a great liberal mind; in the troubled times of the second half of the sixtenth century he was brave enough to write: "I think that the writer is under the obligation of speaking the truth as he sees it." When the freedom of the spirit was completely oppressed by the tyranny of Philip II, he wrote: "The wise man must keep silent these days. . . ." He was honored by the bigot's suspicions and he probably belonged to a circle of influential, highly cultured men who understood that the conflicts of

the sixteenth century were not to be reduced to dogmatic
quarrels but that the stake was the very dignity of the scientist, of the writer, of man. Somewhat disillusioned, he
chose as a motto for his crest, which represented a globe:
"I adorn it, but I despise it."

His claim to glory is that next to Mercator he was the
greatest geographer of his time. He was the first one to
put together the good maps already in circulation, to
which he added several of his own invention, and to publish them in the "most expensive volume of the sixteenth
century," the *Theatre of the World* (1553), which had
three editions in Latin, one in Flemish, several in French
and German—altogether thirty-eight. The book contained
fifty-three maps, and created a world-wide sensation. In
1570 he published a number of additions to his great
work. He was aided by Anna, his sister, who did the color-
ing of the maps, a job that was generally entrusted to
women by the publishers of those days. It had to be done
by hand in order not to obscure the lettering and the other
details of the engraving. His work is scientific and accu-
rate and his commentaries on the regions represented are
still of value. This atlas contains a map of the Americas
that reproduces the rather fantastic ideas geographers had
of that continent. Oddly enough, South America, which
was far better known, looks like a square, while the outline of North America is substantially correct. Except for
part of Canada and a good view of Florida, the whole of
the United States is listed as *terrae incognitae.* The Chamber of Commerce of the orange-blossom state ought to
reprint this map.

Ortelius considered geography "the eye of history." In
his Renaissance eagerness to reconstruct the world of the

ancients, he collected medals and coins, he copied inscriptions and tried with all the scientific means at his disposal to give a correct image of the world as the Romans had seen it. His collection of coins and his publications on that subject made him an authority, and his home became a "must" on the list of the most distinguished sightseers of his time.

Not only did he popularize the study of geography, which was in need of it, but he instigated the drawing of numerous new maps all over Europe. His *Theatrum* is a monument of science, and when he died so many poets took to the pen and the lyre that his friends were obliged to publish a book in his memory, entitled, *Lacrymae Poetarum*—the tears of the poets on the death of Abraham Ortelius. You can always trust the poets; they never shed tears over anybody who isn't really worth while. So let all lovers of atlases, globes and mappemondes join in remembering gratefully April 14 (some say April 4), on which date was born in that pearl of cities, Antwerp, Abraham Ortelius, the father of all the atlases of this vale of tears.

4.—Birth of the Saxophone

WE ARE TOLD THAT THE CHINESE PUT NOUNS AND adjectives one next to the other; they do not connect them. By so doing they save themselves a lot of trouble.

Just see how by the use and abuse of prepositions and conjunctions we complicate life and spoil the best things. Not only do these elements of speech constitute a notorious difficulty for everyone who tries to learn English and who has to remember that one travels *by* train, not *in, on,* or *through* train, but the conjunctions are constantly making havoc by diminishing, altering, or demolishing what one has already said.

We say, "He is a fine man, but he stutters"—which evidently makes him a less fine man. So deficient is our speech that it takes us two clauses of a sentence and a conjunction to express a shade of meaning. We could say, "He is a fine stuttering man," but that would sound like a clinical note, or we could say, "He is a stuttering fine man," and everybody would read a spiritual implication into the phrase and agree that on the road to perfection we all stutter and stumble.

In his exhaustive book, *Belgium,* Hugh Gibson, writing on the lovely Walloon city of Dinant, says: "A certain Mr. Sax, although a respectable burgher, invented the saxophone here." The most important word in this sentence, dangerous and destructive as well, is the conjunction "although." Mr. Sax was a respectable burgher—that is clear—but it is no less clear that Mr. Gibson objects to saxophones; so in the final judgment of this good friend of Belgium, the great man of Dinant does not seem so respectable after all, because he invented the saxophone, which apparently he should not have done. Respectable people do not invent saxophones.

However, the story of Adolph Sax's life shows that the gods, overruling the objections of Mr. Gibson and a great number of other people, wanted Sax to live and invent this instrument. Born on the eve of the battle of Water-loo, he sustained a series of disasters which his biographer has noted down with great accuracy. As a child Sax rolled down the stairs and was bruised so severely that he should have died. He didn't. He swallowed a needle. He lived. He jumped on a burning hot stove. He howled but survived. He drank a generous portion of vitriol; he remained unhurt. He was poisoned by metal fumes; he took arsenic; he came through. A good solid brick fell on his head—it bounced back. And finally he was rescued from drowning. After that they called him "the little ghost from Dinant."

There must be something conducive to herculean deeds in the air of Dinant, for both the outstanding men it produced in the nineteenth century had the same tendency toward gigantism. The painter Adolf Wiertz covered more space with his canvases than anyone known since the Renaissance. His productive genius was constantly hampered by the narrowness of his physical surroundings. Adolph Sax in the realm of music expanded the power and the volume of sounds beyond expectations. One could not say that Wiertz was always a great painter; nor was Sax a great musician, but in a way neither Sax nor Wiertz will be forgotten, for both were gigantic. Both have left their mark on their epoch and will be remembered as having contributed effectively to the arts they practiced.

Dinant is only a small place. Its streets run parallel to the Meuse River, and it is protected by high limestone cliffs from the winds. It has undergone terrible things all through history. In the fifteenth century eight hundred of its menfolk were thrown into the river after a rebellion against the Duke of Burgundy, and in 1914 the Germans destroyed eleven hundred of its fifteen hundred houses, killing seven hundred people, among whom were children under five years of age.

Sax was born there under the shadow of the bulbous-spired church, one of eleven children of a prosperous instrument maker. After studying music in Brussels, he decided to leave for Paris in 1842. He had already a number of small inventions to his credit and, arriving in the capital of France, he wanted to open a workshop to perfect and manufacture them. He started from scratch, and for quite some time he lived in complete poverty, but fame, fortune, and a lot of troubles were in store for him. Several times his earthly possessions were sold, but he kept going, and the most famous musicians and composers of his day patronized and helped him. Meyerbeer called him "the genius of copper and sounding brass," Rossini spoke of the sounds produced by Sax's novelties as of "the most beautiful, sonorous mass" he knew. Donizetti and Halévy supported him, and Bizet used his inventions in the *Suites Arlésiennes*. So did Richard Strauss in his *Symphonia Domestica,* which includes a quartet of saxophones. Debussy wrote a *Rhapsody for Saxophone and Orchestra.*

In 1844 he perfected the most famous of the instruments he was to create—the saxophone. By so doing he achieved for the wind instrument what had long ago been done for the percussion instrument, which had developed from the thin-sounding spinet and harpsichord to the piano. Before his time wind instruments were built on the supposition that the composition of the metal or of the other material determined the timbre of the sound. Sax discovered one of the basic laws of acoustics, that "the proportions given to a column of air vibrating in a sonorous tube, and they alone, determine the character of the timbre produced, not the wall, provided it offers enough resistance." On this basis he was able to develop the volume and the quality of the sound of his instruments to such an extent that he could outplay any combination of instruments and still stay within the boundaries of music and good taste.

His enemies—the other instrument makers—argued that his instruments were "beyond human power." His friends replied that: "Those who first saw the Pyramids thought them to be too high."

In 1845 he had his first decisive triumph: his orchestra was to compete with the most powerful group of his day on the Paris Champ de Mars, a kind of Golden Bowl. His competitor was a Mr. Carafo; the Paris music world was divided between the *Saxons* and the *Carafons*. Sax came out triumphant, and the government made the use of his instrument compulsory for all the military bands of the country. In 1852 he beat with twelve saxtubas of his invention a group of fifteen hundred instruments. Nothing and nobody could outblow or outfanfare the *"cuivres de Sax"* which had become a byword through all Europe. The Revolution of 1848 reverted to less sonorous instruments, but the Emperor Napoleon III reinstalled them. Out of Germany Sax's enemies brought the batyphone, a tube cylindrical in shape except for the bell, to combat his dearest brain child, the saxophone, which was parabolic. The batyphone turned pale and went back to the oblivion of its Teutonic woods. At one time his competitors filed a lawsuit against him to prove that the saxophone did not and even could not exist. But in *La Belle Hélène* Halévy made Ajax rhyme with Sax, and the backbiters of the Belgian sonorous giant were again defeated.

For several decades Sax spent his time fighting off his numerous and unrelenting enemies: he invented several other instruments, perfected scores of existing ones, and got patents for an imposing number of inventions. He was not satisfied even with his musical successes. When the siege of Sebastopol was going on he dreamed of a super-blockbuster which was to be a mortar shell eleven yards wide and weighing five hundred and fifty tons. With one shot this projectile would demolish a whole city. "It would tear apart, smash entire walls, ruin fortifications, explode mines, blow up powerhouses—in a word, exert an irresistible action of devastation, in a wide range, not to mention the horrible fright this explosion will provoke." This weapon would have been called the Saxo-cannon. We have been spared it.

Sax is remembered today, a century after he invented the saxophone, chiefly for this reason and for the saxhorn, the father of a family of brass wind instruments with cup-shaped mouthpieces.

In his famous passage on Christian charity St. Paul speaks in a rather derogatory manner of the "sounding brass." The fact that the saxophone has found such an abundant use in modern jazz music seems to prove that this invention is not absolutely disreputable. The sound it produces certainly does not appertain to the *musica mundana,* the music of the spheres, which the ancients opposed to the *musica humana.* The saxophone has a definitely human and humorous sound; some say its tones are lascivious and therefore reprehensible. Some say "serious" music can do without this Belgian invention. This is irrelevant, since many people can do without "serious" music. But what American orchestra, interpreting the frenzy, the languor, the abdominal uneasiness of our times, could do without the voice of the saxophone, which all of a sudden from among the cacophonic and conflagrating noises of a jazz band rises up and grips us somewhere between the heart and the stomach in a region of our being as yet insufficiently explored, but important and sometimes decisive?

5.—*Damien the Leper*

Recently one of the American Red Cross airplanes was given the name of Father Damien. It was paid for by gifts collected in four Catholic high schools of Honolulu on the occasion of the commemoration of that priest.

What did this Belgian missionary do that his name should go through the skies of the Pacific as an American homage to his life and work?

He was born in 1840 in the village of Tremeloo, Brabant. It is in the Kempen region, a sandy land that has been cultivated and improved for centuries by the sweat and toil of countless generations and transformed into gently rolling, prosperous country. The horizon is low, the country roads are deep and embanked between thick hedges. The villages are like those one sees in Breughel's landscapes: the highway bends slightly before entering the village, as if to slow down traffic and prepare the visitor for a surprise. Always the center of interest, the largest and most impressive building, is the church. It is usually of stone or brick construction, several centuries old, weathered by the frequent rains, venerable and venerated by the parishioners. It has a sharp steeple, carrying a golden cross on top. The slate tiles that cover it are dark blue and, somewhere on the roof, there is a weathervane that creaks and turns, gently pushed around by the winds. The doors of the church are always open, a red light burns in front of the altar, and on entering you pass between the heavy ropes which move the bells, summoning people to the services. Around the church is the graveyard, and on Sunday, after Mass, young and old walk and stand among the graves, reading the names and dates on the tombstones and reminiscing about John and Mary, Paul and Elsie.

In the village, there are a number of cafés, not many, for the peasants have no time on weekdays to go there. A buxom woman stands behind the bar, her white apron stiff with starch, manipulating with authority the handles that dispense the dark or blond beer. Fine white sand is strewn on the red brick floor. The walls are covered with advertisements of sales of land or farm implements: on the yellow posters, the pieces of real estate are marked dark green. There the natives play cards, gossip being left to the women; politics do not excite these people of the land, and tales of marvels in other countries are limited to America and the Congo. For in every village a few daring young people have had the bright idea that apples grow bigger in Canada or in Illinois, that crops grow taller and richer in Michigan than in Flanders, and they have left for those distant lands, sending home some bright colored post cards, coming back on a visit after five years, tanned by the Middle Western sun, prosperous looking, boasting a little and infusing in some of the young minds the nostalgia for foreign eldorados.

The farmers' families are large, and among the sons one at least is supposed to take orders. He will spend some years as assistant priest in a neighboring village, ending his life as curé of his own community, or he will leave for the missions in the Congo, in China, in India, and he may never return. Thousands of young men and women of Belgium have left the peace of their villages, relinquishing the idyllic rural felicity of this comfortable and cozy existence to bring Christianity to the heathen in climates which exhaust their strength and challenge their courage.

The most heroic of them all was undoubtedly Damien de Veuster from Tremeloo, who left his village to become a member of the Picpus missions and at the age of twenty-three was sent to the Sandwich or Hawaii Islands. He was not a very brilliant student, but a plodder, a silent stubborn Fleming who heeded his father's advice: "Words bring familiarity and familiarity is never desirable: with superiors because it is dangerous, with inferiors because it is unbecoming." It took this boy, "Silent Joseph," as he was called by his friends, five months to reach his destination. He was ordained a priest, and started to preach the Christian faith to the Kanakas who lived on the slopes of the volcanoes and who were pleasant fellows altogether had it not been for "their inconstancy and their inconsistency." They imbibed freely and their marital relations were conducted with easy nonchalance and appeared conveniently expandable. They were plagued sometimes by witch doctors and innumerable taboos from which Father Damien, a husky, aggressive man of the Lord, definitely freed them, sometimes using physical violence to destroy the fetishes.

The arrival of the white man had brought to the Hawaii archipelago the horrible plague of leprosy, and the local potentates had found no other solution but to exile all the lepers to Molokai island, where these human wrecks were supposed to act as colonists and to care for themselves. The result was what might have been expected: the "colony" became an inferno of suffering, of drinking and wild debauchery in an atmosphere of putrefaction and death. When the Bishop of the islands asked for a volunteer among his priests to go to Molokai and tend to the lepers, to go and stay there for the rest of his life, he chose Damien from among the four candidates. The priest had to start from scratch. The first night he "lit a pipe, leaned against a tree trunk, thinking"—so he writes —and he may well have thought deeply because he had, at the age of thirty-three, arrived at the gates of Hades, among the horrible grimacing shadows of a group of eight hundred drunken and debauched moribunds who used to tell newcomers: "In this place there is no law." He did the sensible thing, first tackling the horrible living conditions in the settlement: he built a water supply system, he helped to erect three hundred houses, he planted gardens, he protected these poor people, who were all waiting for death in two or three years, from themselves.

There was no doctor; he became their doctor; there was no carpenter; he made the coffins; he was the gravedigger and the dietitian, the mason and the advocate. He built a church and a hospital. He was the confidant and the confessor and finally among the lepers he became one of them, contracting that horrible disease which the Egyptians called so vividly "death before death."

One day, saying Mass, he discovered the symptoms of the malady on his skin and when he was to address the congregation, did not say "My Brethren," as usual, but spoke slowly and said: "We, lepers. . . ." When the lepers wanted to frighten people they used to rush up to them and embrace them, putting their open sores against a healthy body. Never had they done that to their great and admired friend the Belgian priest, but Damien had never feared contamination. In order to win the confidence of his parishioners he had eaten with them and given them his pipe to smoke. In his absence, they slept in his bed and browsed around his hut.

At the age of forty-five, Damien entered the portals of death with a smile. To a doctor he declared: "I would not have my health restored to me at the price of my having to leave the island and abandon my work here." Soon he became disfigured. His nose was swollen, his ears out of shape. He lost one eye, he tottered as he walked, his voice became hoarse and weak, his hands were mere stumps. After four years, he felt death approaching. His assistant spoke to him: "Leave me your mantle, that like Elias, I may inherit your great heart," but Damien rejected this homage and replied: "It is full of leprosy."

He had been isolated on Molokai for many years, but the world had heard of his bravery and his sacrifice. In

London, the Prince of Wales, later King Edward VII, said:

"The heroic life and death of Father Damien has not only roused the sympathy of the United Kingdom, but it has gone deeper—it has brought home to us that the circumstances of our vast Indian and Colonial Empire oblige us, in a measure at least, to follow his example."

The greatest of the earth gave him praise and, when one small dissenting voice was heard, it so provoked the wrath of the great author Robert Louis Stevenson, that it inspired one of the most beautiful defenses ever written.

In 1936, the remains of Father Damien were brought back to Belgium. They traveled on an American man-of-war to San Francisco. They were brought into the harbor of Antwerp on the three-masted barkentine "Mercator," the training ship of the Belgian navy. Damien returned to his convent in Louvain, whence he had left, a young, eager but humble brother, unknown to the world. On his return, on the quay, King and Cardinal waited for him to pay tribute to one who had so generously, so bravely, made the supreme sacrifice and, as the Gospel says, had "laid down his life for his friends."

6.—*Ulenspiegl*

THE MOST OUTSTANDING CHARACTERISTIC OF BELGIUM'S intellectual and cultural life is the fact that the country constitutes the point of intersection between two great cultures—the Latin and the Germanic. Ethnologically, the Belgian population is about equally divided between French- and Dutch-speaking people, and is thus exposed to French or Germanic influence. But while French thought finds little or no difficulty in penetrating into the southern part of Belgium and into its capital, Brussels, the influence of German culture has always been obstructed by the fact that the difference between the German and the Dutch languages is far from negligible.

In the development of European culture, Belgium, even before it achieved political and national unity, was a buffer state. It absorbed the shock between two sensibilities, two conceptions of life which otherwise might have rudely conflicted. Before the rise of nationalism, which is based mainly on a mystic reverence for the binding element of a common language, the problem of cultural competition and spheres of intellectual influence in Europe was quite different from what it is today. At that time Belgium was not sandwiched in between powerfully unified states, which tried to drag her in their orbits. In the Middle Ages and even as late as the sixteenth century, the political and economic position of the Lowlands in western Europe was of such prominence that far from being influenced by cultural imperialism, Holland and Belgium were the center of a radiation which spread over all Europe. As the political and economic significance of Belgium declined after her separation from Holland, the cultural picture changed too, and Belgium only reasserted herself intellectually from the moment she regained her independence. This much can be said for nationalism: that it encourages a culture to express itself with the utmost vigor, with supreme clarity and self-confidence. Among minor exponents of the nationalistic creed, this leads sometimes to a ridiculous overestimation, but in exceptional cases, it may produce outstanding achievements.

Those who believe in the inevitable recurrence of spiritual as well as political events will find comfort in the fact that in the Middle Ages a uniform conception of Christianity, an identical understanding of life and death, resulted in a hallucinatory identity between artistic and spiritual expression and that, after a long interlude of progressive, acute nationalism and even aggressive provincialism, the world reverts to a mode of expression which has that same urge toward universality and internationalism which was the most precious achievement of what only the bigoted call the dark Middle Ages.

There is little waste in the artistic and intellectual fields. Even the most extreme and clumsy experiments have their function and significance. Every literary movement, every intellectual tendency seems to be part of a Brownian movement which we may observe, even without being able to foresee its final role. Nationalistic feeling, however absurd from a philosophical standpoint, however ridiculous in its often unjustified assumptions of its own excellence and superiority, has inspired and produced works of art in all fields which have enriched not only the country that gave birth to them, but which have finally become part of the spiritual treasure of civilized man, regardless of language and nationality.

The rebirth of an independent Belgium in the nineteenth century inspired two books of universal value and wide popularity—*The Lion of Flanders,* by Hendrik Conscience, and *The Glorious Adventures of Tyl Ulenspiegl,* by Charles de Coster.

To refute all claims of racial purity and nationalistic integrity, it may be noted that the man who did most to revive and encourage the Flemings' pride in their history and language was the son of a French official who had come to Antwerp to help build the ships with which Napoleon was to invade England. In the best tradition of Sir Walter Scott, Conscience wrote his Bible of Flemish belief, *The Lion of Flanders*. It is a romantic, powerful, epic tale of the defeat of the French aristocracy by the Flemish urban democracies. Written in 1838, it was translated into a great number of languages, and its American edition still belongs on the preferred reading list of romantic youngsters. The American preface says: "With this novel, Conscience won his place in the literature of the world, which he held to the end of his busy career. He was hailed as a great author by all Europe."

The second book is De Coster's *Ulenspiegl*. De Coster was neither Flemish nor Walloon; he was born in Brussels, where he spent most of his life. He had a very poor knowledge of Flemish, but his book became the very compendium of everything Flemish. He wrote in French, but whenever foreign critics refer to his masterpiece, they seldom mention that he used French to express himself, and English as well as German essayists generally speak of De Coster as a Flemish writer. This goes to show that language is not such an absolute factor as the nationalists of all countries pretend. Nobody has written about Flanders more lovingly, more tenderly and with deeper enthusiasm than De Coster; no book ever written anywhere has done more to bring out one side of the Flemish character and make the world love it.

Tyl Ulenspiegl is in a class with *Don Quixote* and Rabelais' *Pantagruel*. As is the case with many great works of world literature, the author did not create his type. Goethe got his theme for Faust in a popular tale. De Coster was inspired by another folk story that had wide circulation in Germany and the Lowlands for more than seven centuries—the tale of Tyl Ulenspiegl, a sympathetic knave, a practical joker, an indirect moralist, pretending to be naïve or a fool in order to show other people their folly and their weaknesses. The original Ulenspiegl is nothing more than a Rabelaisian gaybird. De Coster made him the symbol of the popular spirit of resistance in the Lowlands during the sixteenth century. Ulenspiegl's father is burned at the stake for heresy and Ulenspiegl carries his father's ashes in a pouch on his breast. He is told to avenge this crime. He becomes the embodiment of the popular movement of revolt and hatred against the Spaniards and what they stood for. The reformed have everyone and everything against them— weapons, the law, the Church. They have only their wits and their courage to help them. Tyl has both, together with a refreshing sense of humor. Writing with forceful simplicity, De Coster created a Philip of Spain who is about the most revolting sadist one can imagine, but if there were no real historic truth in Tyl, why should there have been in Philip?

The Spaniards in Flanders wanted to maintain the Catholic religion, they wanted to impose a 10 per cent tax on revenue, they wanted to force the municipal authorities to bow to their centralizing tactics. Therefore, they burned heretics, they confiscated their goods, they imprisoned and even executed those they considered dangerous to the regime. On a smaller scale they gave a pretty good preview of totalitarianism in action.

The people of the Lowlands refused to accept such treatment. They revolted, some on religious grounds, others—the majority—for political reasons. The war lasted many years. It ended in the defeat of the southern Netherlands, Belgium, which was returned to Spanish rule, and also in the independence of the United Provinces of Holland. De Coster tells the story of this revolt and the south's subsequent defeat, not from the standpoint of the leaders, but from that of the humble artisan, of the obscure saboteur, and of the devoted soldier. His book gives a picture of Belgian life and manners in the sixteenth century as rich as a colorful tapestry and as irresistibly amusing, but the main theme is the revolt of free man against tyranny, against those who tell him what to believe and what not to believe, and who will kill him if he chooses the wrong dogma. His hero is an individualistic democrat, endowed with a vigorous appetite for life in all its aspects, a sensualist and at the same time a primitive partisan. His opinions are not based on political or metaphysical reasoning; he feels what is wrong and fights against it.

Readers, therefore, in Russia as well as in Germany, in Spain as well as in Italy, in Iceland as well as in Hungary, have loved this book that exalts above all the land of Flanders, Brabant and Walloonia. What was meant to be the voice of a small group of men has become the echo of millions of free souls all over the globe.

7.—*Death Came to the Cardinal*

ON JANUARY 23, 1926, CARDINAL DÉSIRÉ MERCIER, PRImate of Belgium, died. If he had been only a distinguished churchman of that small country, his departure would have caused little enough sensation.

It is an old rule that cardinals die as well as shopkeepers and policemen. In Louis XIII's time Malherbe found out that even the beautiful wrought-iron gates of the Louvre could not keep Death out of the royal palace. Before him the painters and engravers of the fifteenth century had taken visible pleasure in portraying kings, cardinals and bishops, as well as rich people and beautiful women at grips with a flute-playing skeleton, leading them all to their final mortal destruction. Death comes for the archbishop as it comes for anybody else. But we are so constituted that every time we hear of the death of a man who stood out above his fellow men, who seemed to be possessed of a power and a vitality unusual among his contemporaries, we can scarcely believe it, even if he had reached the Biblical three score and ten which, theoretically at least, we allot to every man.

That happened when Cardinal Mercier died. Prostrate Europe was still bandaging its wounds, a frenzy of sensuality was sweeping over the whole world. People were still trying to make up for the privations and misery of the long war by grasping everything in their reach and looking frantically for new means of asserting their vitality. Those who had been heroes in the fight, living in the exaltation produced by the constant threat of deadly danger, had finally adapted themselves to the drudgery of a peaceful existence. After the Napoleonic wars it took the youth of Europe more than ten years to forget that they had roamed the world like demigods in search of herculean works to perform, to settle down and watch their waistlines expand comfortably, fatally, humiliatingly.

At such an euphoric moment Mercier died, reminding people that international happiness, global prosperity and cosmic well-being were only recent acquisitions of mankind, reminding them too that all this might be only a temporary state and that the very basis of life must be a constant vigilance and readiness to sacrifice.

He had been a Catholic priest for forty-two years, which was not unusual. He had been a promoter of Thomistic philosophy, and philosophers and theologians knew of him as such and of his ardent defense of Aquinas' monumental work and writings, of his endeavor to reconcile scholastic thought and modern science, to wipe out the alleged antithesis between metaphysical belief and technical reality, to break down the barriers between religion and science. In that field, in the spirit of strictest Catholic orthodoxy, he had done what the philosophers of all tendencies—even his fiercest enemies—were to do at the end of the nineteenth and during the first half of the twentieth century. But little of all that could have entitled him to universal popularity. The layman who in the nineteenth century had heard many outstanding scientists proclaim the grossest kind of materialism was not overwhelmingly surprised to hear half a century later that most of them agreed that behind the external world there existed a moving principle, that life was not accidental.

Mercier's international popular fame was due to the role he played in the First World War. He embodied the right of the spirit against the vileness of brute force. He stood up against the Germans and forced them to the recognition that—in the words of the German governor of Belgium in 1918—he was the "revered spiritual leader of the Belgian people."

This tribute was worth all the more to those who knew Belgium well. For the outside world Belgium is a "Catholic country" because the majority of the Belgians profess that religion, but like any other traditionally Catholic nation in Europe, it had a powerful group recruited mostly from among the intellectual and scholastic people who did not belong to the Church. They were greatly outnumbered by the Catholic majority, but their spiritual influence was much wider than their limited numbers might lead one to conclude. If the German governor gave Mercier this extraordinary homage, it was not on account of the fact that the Cardinal was a Catholic primate; on the contrary, it happened in spite of this special circumstance.

The Church and the state in Belgium are separated; the state subsidizes all creeds on the same basis, Protestant, Jewish or Catholic, but there is no state religion, and both the state and the Church jealously guard their domains against each other's interference.

During the last war, as during the present one, the Belgian authorities were outside Belgium, fighting on for their country; in Belgium only a few high officials, the local mayors and aldermen were left. The Church was the only national organization to stay intact, although a great number of priests were murdered by the invaders. Thus from the beginning Cardinal Mercier spoke up in the name of the majority of his countrymen and, later on, he had the entire country behind him. In his pastoral letters, "Patriotism and Endurance," and others, he expounded the thesis that the Belgians owed neither respect nor allegiance to the occupant, that they should not obey the Germans in anything that would be detrimental to the fatherland. He protested violently against the burning of Louvain, he rose to the height of eloquence when he accused Germany of the deportation of about 50,000 Belgian workmen. When the Germans tried to split the country morally by playing politics, he raised his voice, expressing the reaction of silenced Belgian public opinion.

He never despaired of Belgium's cause. As early as 1916 he wrote and had the text read in all the churches: "The moral triumph of Belgium in the eyes of civilization and history is already an accomplished fact." Through the darkest hours of the war he never faltered, and the resonance of his words—which the enemy could never stop— was greater than anything the Germans could say in Belgium.

For four years he fought a duel with the invader. Every injustice, every brutality the occupying power committed, he attacked and denounced, and since he was a gifted writer, a keen logician, and altogether a powerful mind and persuasive personality, his words carried far more effect than the invader's clumsy replies and stammered excuses. In a time of national distress he had become the spokesman of the nation.

It was one of the most dramatic moments of patriotic fervor in Belgium when Cardinal Mercier officiated in the age-old cathedral of St. Gudula in Brussels, when his frail and emaciated figure appeared in the pulpit and his voice resounded under the dark brown Gothic arches of the church. It was one of the highlights of the restored peace when in 1920 General Pershing, passing by in a victory parade on Fifth Avenue and seeing Cardinal Mercier in the grandstand, dismounted to greet the prelate of a small and martyred nation.

As Churchill electrified the British nation by the mere power of his word and of his personality, so Cardinal Mercier, when Belgium's position seemed completely hopeless, gave his compatriots an absolute confidence in their national future. Later, when the enemy tried to destroy Belgium, he became technically and morally the *defensor civitatis,* the defender of the community, like those bishops of old who left the protecting walls of their cities to encounter the murderous barbarians and who by the dignity of their office and their personal prestige often succeeded in quelling the pagan hordes.

The good men do is not always "interred with their bones." Fortunately not. In the case of Cardinal Mercier, it is quite certain that his example has inspired his successor and his countrymen during this war, that wherever a brave man in Belgium has lifted his voice in protest against the obscenities of Nazism, the spirit of this brave and great man has hovered over him.

8.—*One Man Dies*

Roughly speaking, the nine provinces which compose present-day Belgium correspond to the duchies, counties and ecclesiastical principalities which through the ages evolved from a group of aristocratic possessions to become a democratic, united country. The only souvenir of these feudal origins is the custom of giving medieval titles to the members of the royal family. For the rest, the former county of Flanders, the marquisate of Antwerp, the principality of Liége and the county of Namur are just administrative units of the Belgian state.

They each have a governor, who is not a delegate of the people nor an elected officer, but who is a representative of the King in his province. He is not a politician, he is an official, supposed to be the moderator of the provincial counsel, the maintainer of the legal traditions and laws. His powers are relatively small; his moral position is comparatively high. Being appointed for life, as a rule he becomes an element of conciliation and of peace.

There are no definite rules which determine the choice

of the governors whose appointments have to be presented by the Minister of the Interior to the King for approval. Although in most cases a governorship is far from being a sinecure, only sedate people have generally been selected for these nine posts. Traditionally they had been given to the representatives of the local nobility, but that tradition was scrapped after the last war. Instead of looking for the social prestige to be derived from the presence of an elderly nobleman as governor, the government preferred to entrust the public affairs of the provinces to younger men who had been trained in different services or who had taken part in politics. A craving for efficiency took the place of reverence for archaeology.

But still something solemn, a little outmoded, remained the attribute of this office. The governors were housed in venerated old buildings, most of the time in premises which had been built by bishops in the seventeenth or eighteenth centuries. Reception rooms were enormous, with beautiful white-and-black checkered floors. Elaborate chandeliers threw just enough light in the age-tarnished mirrors of the salons not to show too clearly the gold stucco crumbling from the ceilings where cupids and nymphs had circled for centuries around a benevolent Neptune or a not overchaste Venus.

It was fitting that in such surroundings the host should be properly decorative. A heavy gold-braided uniform was the governor's dress on solemn occasions. Thus attired he greeted the King and distinguished visitors; thus, following the Holy Sacrament, he marched through the crooked streets around the old cathedrals when on big feast days a religious procession wound through the town. His functions were manifold, his duties varied and delicate. His influence was often challenged or even combated by the mayor of one or another of the big cities in his domain. These representatives of the people permitted only with reluctance his interference in communal affairs. But the many smaller communities were entrusted to his special care. He watched over their finances, instigating the government to provide for public utilities, urging the urbanization of districts which had lost their rural character. The governor could, and usually did, accomplish many useful things in this way.

But every function is what the man who exercises it makes of it. There were in Belgium insignificant governors and brilliant ones: some were solemn and boring like rain on Sunday; others were scholarly men and great administrators; still others had literary tendencies. Those belonging to the last category not only took good care of the interests of their domain, but they became its bards, its singers. So enthusiastic could they become about their small territory that they were ready to sing its praises with a love so exclusive as to push the rest of the world into the background.

Such was François Bovesse, Governor of Namur Province. The domain he ruled is one of the most picturesque parts of Walloonia: a dozen lovely rivers rush through it, winding through narrow green valleys; there is Dinant, on which Wilhelm II wept two beautiful crocodile tears, his army having destroyed it and murdered its inhabitants; and there are also the grottoes of Han, "bigger and better" than the Kentucky caves; there are scores of old castles and citadels on strategic heights, recalling fierce fights in feudal times; and there is Namur, the capital, where people assert their closeness to Latinity by calling one of their avenues "Boulevard ad aquam." Legends flourish in this country, gracefully and abundantly.

Governor Bovesse was born there. In the last war he was in the front lines and sustained a severe wound. He entered politics and became Minister of Education. He was an ardent defender of the cultural patrimony of the Walloon country. Having abandoned his early ambition to become an actor, he used his resonant basso in the defense of the ideas of the Liberal Party. He was a charming man, a good mixer, of ready wit, and even when using the beautiful organ tones of his booming voice to create an effect of pathos, he was still sympathetic and delightful. After fifteen years in Parliament, he was appointed Governor of Namur Province. He devoted some of his time to poetry and became the poet of the Meuse river. The beauty of the Walloon countryside inspired him, and gave to every one of his public utterances a warmth and a lyrical quality which was quite unusual in public life. It was one of the colorful events in Belgian circles when this man stood up after dinner, resting from time to time with his hand on the table, because of his physical handicap and, before people who had heard him many times already, spoke of the valleys, streams and grottoes of the Namur country. For a few minutes the hellhounds of politics quieted down to listen attentively to the siren song of a man profoundly in love with the land of his birth, to which he was giving all his energy and a measureless devotion.

According to his instructions, he left Belgium in 1940 after the invasion and was in charge of the Belgian refugees in Sète, France. He went back to his country and was savagely attacked and physically molested by the Fascists, who had some old grudge against this firm believer in freedom and democracy. The Nazis, of course, prevented him from resuming his duties as governor, and he would certainly have objected to serving them. He stayed in Namur as a private citizen, but his very presence angered his enemies. So well did he embody the spirit of Namur that every act of resistance in the province was interpreted by them as inspired by this brave man. In 1941 they succeeded in having him arrested and sentenced to six months in prison, which he served in Brussels.

Early one morning, four unknown men called at his home. The maid refused to let the callers disturb her master. Mr. Bovesse heard the discussion. He walked downstairs, wishing to confront the intruders. They fired on the defenseless man: he died. The four assassins left. Next day their press insulted the memory of that good citizen, that brave soldier, that distinguished patriot.

In the course of this global war, this crime is but a minor incident. A middle-aged man falls down the stairs of his home, riddled with bullets. He leaves a widow and two children. One man dies. On the European fronts thousands of young soldiers fall every day. What sense is there in underlining the murder in an obscure provincial town of Belgium of a former official of that country?

Fighting armies are followed by war correspondents who tell us a few hours after the events how the battle proceeded, who sing the praise of the heroes. We see and meet brave men who came back from the front to tell us their story. The armies are articulate, heroism is no longer obscure. But out of an occupied country news filters sparingly. Hundreds of people die with scarcely anybody hearing of their fate. Most of them are humble citizens, craftsmen, plain honest men who could not swallow their disgust at the Nazi regime, who talked or behaved patriotically and therefore died. This time one of the highest officials of the country fell in the battle of Belgium. It meant that the defeated Fascist Party had seen the handwriting on the wall. It meant that like the captive tiger they felt themselves caged behind the bars of national hatred, overshadowed by the coming disaster to Germany's might.

Seeing the twilight of their gods, they wanted to take vengeance on those who were morally responsible for its coming. They killed wantonly, savagely, cravenly. In the moment that François Bovesse died, a martyr was born, and all his many friends both inside and outside Belgium understood from this terroristic action that victory had come one step closer, that her sweet face had become more distinct through the mist of the raging battle.

IV

CHRONICLE
OF OPPRESSION

1.—The Quill Drivers' Field Day

As a rule the European government official is not a very inspiring kind of person. He is rightly supposed to be serious, unimaginative and dry. Most of the time he is, and how could he be otherwise? He chose his career; he decided that he would be one of the cogs in the governmental machinery. One could ask: who wants to be a cog? He does. From the start he accepted the fact that whatever his place in the administration, he would have somebody above him to tell him what to do and especially what to avoid. He decidedly renounced the opportunity of being his own master in life, of enjoying that feeling of independence and invigorating instability that free enterprise brings. He wanted to be a public servant, a servant of the anonymous, multitudinous public, but in fact he became the servant of his immediate superior. This superior, this man of experience and standing, is, of course, middle-aged or old. His waistline has expanded, he is paying the last installment of the mortgage on his house, he economizes to send his no-good son to college and to buy a decent winter coat for his daughter. A sedentary life has given him a permanent stomach or liver ailment. He is disillusioned and, therefore, often a little bitter.

The young official asks himself if this man still believes in his task. Does he see any grandeur in being a public servant and the chief of a number of younger people who will take over when he retires or dies from his stomach ulcer? He rarely does, for idealism is most of the time the privilege and burden of youth. When this man entered administration, he felt just like the young official and said: "I am different from the man who wants to sell the greatest possible number of toothbrushes or refrigerators; *he* is an egoist, an opportunist, *he* is a money chaser; it is revolting and humiliating to hear him speak of his toothbrushes and refrigerators as if he were performing an invaluable service to mankind, while I am part of an organization men have invented and perfected for hundreds of centuries to foster the general good: the government, the utmost achievement of civilization.

"I will protect the weak and check the powerful. I will be just. I will hold the balance between conflicting interests. I will partake—modestly, of course—of the distribution of justice in this world. I will avoid red tape. I will work swiftly and effectively. I will devote myself entirely to the good of the public."

Of course, only a small part of this magnificent program materialized. In his youth, the mediocrity of his material existence did not weigh very heavily on him, but, as life went on, he began to see that his idealistic conception of his humble task was submitted to a terrible strain. He discovered that most of the older men in the service had become skeptical and even cynical, that responsibility was so divided and scattered that finally, even if everybody did his duty, catastrophes would happen and blunders could not be avoided. He saw that many of these men had finally discovered that they were only cogs in a vast ponderous machinery, and that, in the secret of their hearts, they had concluded that the greatness of life to which, like all other humans, they were entitled, lay elsewhere, outside the walls of their drab offices. In amazement, and later on in panic, he discovered that many of those performing the official rites were secretly heretics for whom the service had become just a means of making a meager living.

This moment constitutes the dramatic climax of the official's career, the turning point of his life, his administrative menopause, his solemn chance for that self-destruction and rebirth through fear and pity which in the Greek drama is called the Catharsis. He has to decide then if for the rest of his life he will be one of those dull stiff-collared unimaginative quill drivers, one of those old stick-in-the-muds who frighten and terrorize orderly citizens by their humorless and repulsive aspect, who die of old age, of discontent and the smallness of their pension. Or he will overcome all that. Discarding the mediocrity and frailness of human nature, he will go back to the faith of his youth and decide that being a public servant is something like being a priest. He will find his satisfaction and his glory in the distribution of justice, in that daily, difficult task of deciding between interests, refusing to be impressed by those who have the money and the power, or unduly depressed by those who have only their weakness and their tears to defend them in the world.

We are told—even by the greatest enemies of the Soviet regime—that the real believers in the Soviet system are not very numerous but are animated by a solemn faith in their task, imposing upon themselves both restraint and discipline, in order to realize what they consider an ideal society. They are not, we are told, after riches, after caviar and mink coats; they are striving for a society which would be the realization of their dreams and, in order to attain it, they impose upon themselves a number of restrictions and limitations which, in a Christian world, are only inspired by the spirit of mortification.

The ideal government official in any government has some of that spirit. In times like these, officials everywhere in Europe and in occupied Asia have been put on trial. A number of them have proved to be only human—that is, weak, fickle and inconsistent, thinking essentially of their own small interests, of their careers and their safety, but for the honor of officialdom, many of them, especially among the higher ranks, have had the one occasion of their life to prove their mettle and to give testimony of their belief in their task.

Many such cases have occurred in Belgium. In most instances, however, it is rather difficult to explain where and how they gave those proofs of bravery and greatness. Administrative dramas—such things do exist—are always very complicated and difficult to analyze. But, fortunately, there are some cases when all of a sudden things become simple and clear.

One recent example was given by the Government Audit Department in Belgium. The gentlemen working there are professional wet blankets. The Constitution orders them to check on all expenses incurred by the state. For any enterprising minister they are a nightmare. They see that expenses do not run over the amount allotted by the budget, and they prevent credits from being transferred from one section to another, which constitutes the great and inevitable temptation in administrative life. They are as annoying as indispensable individuals in a state government can be. Nobody loves them, and in peacetime it is a fair guess that they did not even like themselves very much. Among Belgian officials, theirs was the most thankless job—that of being bogeyman to all and sundry.

When the Germans started organizing the New Order in Belgium, they found very few officials willing to take their orders. They dismissed some, promoted others and appointed several of their admirers to high posts. But one cannot effectively fight an unyielding body of men without destroying the entire organization. Therefore, the Germans decided to leave the indispensable ministries alone, but to create, in close touch with them and practically in control of them, a number of boards and agencies which were entirely organized according to German wishes and needs. Of course, this subterfuge was illegal from the Belgian standpoint. The funds these agencies used and lived on came from the department, but everything was done in a cozy way, without interference from "strangers."

The Government Audit Department had warned the responsible officials several times that nobody was allowed to spend government money without submitting an account to its scrutiny and approval. The German-organized agencies turned a deaf ear to these entreaties. Things went on for quite some time until the gentlemen of the Audit Department lost their patience. They went to court and requested that a number of officials in charge of important bureaus be sued and heavily fined for refusing to obey the laws of the country. The court went to work and delivered the summons.

The rest of the story followed a familiar pattern. The Germans stepped in and put some of the members of the Audit Department in jail. They even thought of dismissing the whole department. The German officials continued to spend all the money their friends gave them, without control and without publicity, according to the system of the totalitarian regime. But once more a group of honest, simple and brave men had done its duty. In pagan days the test of faith was martyrdom. In occupied countries, the proof of decency is a German sentence to jail.

2.—*"That Which Diverts and Makes Mirth"*

NOAH WEBSTER SAYS—AND WHO WOULD DARE TO CONtradict him?—that sport is "that which diverts and makes mirth." Thus, contrary to what some people seem to believe, he does not claim that sport is a kind of religion, a lifetime occupation or a profession. It is always a good idea to listen to Mr. Webster, Noah.

If at a gathering of Belgians before the war someone had stood up and asked, "Is there a sportsman in the house?" he would have been met by silence, for no Belgian has ever taken sports seriously enough to confess that he spent most of his time "diverting himself and making mirth."

Sport in prewar Belgium was a pastime, an honorable one indeed, but one on which serious people looked a bit askance.

Notwithstanding this reserved attitude, the Belgians excelled in several forms of sport. They played soccer beautifully, they swam well, and when they got hold of a bicycle, few people in Europe could keep up with them.

Football never became a national sport, but local soccer teams were very popular. Soccer was not the exclusive privilege of college boys; it belonged to everybody, rich or poor, young or old, and the half center and goalkeepers who, on Sunday afternoon, would kick the ball sky-high, or slip in the mud of a rain-soaked field defending the goal, would sit on Monday morning behind the cashier's desk at a bank or defend the widow and the orphan in court.

The major event of the soccer year was the match between Holland and Belgium, held alternately in Rotterdam and in Antwerp. Thousands of Dutchmen used to invade Antwerp on that occasion, and all the café and restaurant owners in town treacherously implored the gods that Holland might win, for in that event the Dutchmen would paint the town red for a night. If they lost, they would steal noiselessly back to their canals without profiting the Antwerp liquor trade at all.

But bicycling was the real national craze. It could go on any time, anywhere, in winter as well as in summer. Over the long flat roads of Flanders, boys in their teens would race home from school on their bicycles, farmhands and bricklayers would crouch over the handle bars, streamlining themselves against the strong winds which bend the poplars and the elms permanently toward the northwest.

Every village carnival included a bicycle race, and some towns would suddenly get on the map for having discovered a perfect figure-eight circuit for bicycle contests. The champions rated as high in popularity as any American baseball star. In recent years even girl racers became well known in the field. The most famous contest, however, was the circuit of France held every year. It was followed by the entire Belgian population—even by those who usually did not care for sports—with breathless anxiety. As a rule, Belgian national pride was upheld and one could be certain that the Belgians would be foremost among the winners. With the money won in France the champion usually settled down, married a sweet plump girl from his home town, opened a café and spent the rest of his life talking about the way he climbed the Pyrenees or the time his tires blew out on the outrageous cobblestones of the industrial cities of northern France.

Once a year in the hills of Walloonia, automobile races were held at Francorchamps, and the daredevils of both hemispheres would risk their lives with complete nonchalance. Some people played tennis, a few played golf, but one can safely say that a large percentage of sporting people in Belgium never took part in any sport at all, except by getting their feet wet on the edge of a soccer field or shouting themselves hoarse to encourage the demigods of the bicycle. Most of the Belgians were merely sport fans.

After the Germans invaded Belgium, they tried to take over and regulate sports for their own political purposes. There were two major organizations in existence—the

Olympic Committee and the Belgian Federation of Sports Associations. The Germans tried to win over both and to incorporate them in their "New Order" policy. But before long, strong opposition arose, and guerrilla warfare broke out between the Quisling administration, acting for the Germans, and the different sports associations. The main reason for the conflict was that the Nazis wanted to divide sports activities along linguistic lines, which was not only contrary to the associations' traditional policy but absurd from a practical standpoint. When the local associations tried to organize interurban bicycle races, the Quislings intervened and ordered certain mayors to forbid the races from taking place on their territories. When soccer matches were held in defiance of Nazi orders, the Germans dispersed the crowds by charging onto the soccer fields with their cavalry. Chaos ensued.

In Germany, sports have been a means of influencing public opinion. The display of well-trained athletic men and women was supposed to prove in some way the greatness of the Nazi regime, as well as its youthful vigor. Sport served the Cause and therefore was a weapon. The Belgians did not want a peaceful pastime to become a political instrument. They were fed up with "ersatzes" and they insisted on taking their sports straight. Difficulties of transportation and communication in occupied Belgium made national competitions impossible. Only the federations controlled by the Nazis were in a position to organize contests of that kind, but the Belgians boycotted these matches, and most of the time the collaborationist sportsmen displayed their skill before empty benches.

Sports activities are greatly handicapped by the physical condition of the Belgian population. In September, 1942,

a Dutch weekly reported that within the short period of
two days, three boxers in Belgium had been killed in the
ring. Since they were young people, this seems to indicate
that their power of resistance was extremely low. The paper reported that in many instances dope had been used in
sports events and that a great number of players had been
crippled for life on account of the practices employed by
the Germans or by the managers of the sports matches.

Under the pretense that life had returned to normal in
Belgium, the Germans insisted on having Belgian sportsmen participate in international events, evidently with a
political purpose in mind. The Olympic Committee in
charge of this matter issued an order to all its members,
forbidding them to take part in sports events outside
Belgium and especially in Germany. Most of the associations followed this example, to the great dismay of the
Germans.

Confronted with this opposition, the Nazis decided
that the time had come to organize Belgian sport, and
they appointed a sports commissioner from among their
Rexist friends. They chose Pierre Daye, a newspaperman
and former Rexist deputy, whose main contribution to
sport in the past had been the fact that he had once belonged to a group of nudists. He eagerly accepted this
new job, although even the Quisling newspapers stated
that the field of his proposed activities was entirely new to
him. His appointment was preceded by a remarkable incident. The Olympic Committee got hold of the order creating the sports commission a few weeks before it was
published. It distributed this document to all sports organizations, urging them to oppose it and not to recognize
either Pierre Daye or his organization.

The Olympic Committee summoned the representatives of all the sports associations and submitted a formal proposal that all sports activities should cease, in protest against the decrees of the German Sports Commissioner. This proposal was accepted, and the various Belgian sports associations published their decision to refuse all contact with the officials of the sports commission and to forbid their clubs and members to take part in any public sports event. The Quisling press interpreted this decision as "tantamount to a declaration of war on the Commission."

When the Nazis say that Nazism is a philosophy which influences and changes the aspect of every human activity in the state, they are perfectly right. Indeed, wherever they can, they apply the idea that the individual is essentially a part of the state and that his every act should be of service to the nation, i.e., the Nazi machine. No human values escape the contamination of Nazism. In the occupied countries, the task of all decent people has been to repel these attacks wherever they occurred.

Before the war, it was a standing rule in Belgium that local sports associations, even those devoted to the innocent pastime of dart throwing or pigeon races, should proclaim in the first paragraph of their by-laws that they were "buiten en boven alle politiek" (beyond and above politics). It is the irony of fate that under the German regime this rather ridiculous and innocent declaration of principle should have become the expression of human decency in the face of tyranny.

3.—*"Tiesses di Hoye"*

FOR AGES PEOPLE HAVE PRAYED FOR THOSE "WHO GO down to the sea in ships." This special devotion reflects some of the horror and awe the watery part of the world inspired in primitive man. The Greeks, the most seafaring of all ancient peoples, seldom spoke of the sea with that nautical enthusiasm the moderns who have mastered her dangers usually display. For those who go down into the earth there is no special prayer, although when Orpheus descends to Hades he pleads with the "specters, furies, horrid shades" who defend the entrance to the underworld. But after all, he was on a special errand. We are told that those who wanted to make their abode in the sky and thus depart from the earth were stricken with utter confusion at Babel; man is not supposed to inhabit the sky; he may only pass through.

The first men who went down into the crust of the earth, to reach for its riches, must have felt terror. They must have experienced the same feeling of transgressing on a domain that was forbidden to them and therefore dangerous. For as soon as man leaves his natural habitat, not only do practical problems arise, but he is also confronted with a number of questions which challenge his normal moral conduct, the idea he has about his final destiny, the reasons he found for his existence and his actions.

There is something about a miner that distinguishes him from other workers, that puts him in a class apart. The fact that he spends most of his time away from the sun, its lovely light, its penetrating warmth, confers on him a kind of asceticism; the fact that he does a dangerous job helps to enhance his dignity as a worker. He is alone a great deal, constantly threatened by the tunnels caving in, and menaced by darkness. He has time to think about what makes things move, and he finds out that even within the bosom of the earth there is no real comfort.

Therefore it is probably not a mere accident that the eloquence of John L. Lewis is essentially Biblical in inspiration: the solemnity of his pronouncements intended for the miners must have a special appeal to them on that account. The Welsh miners are known for their deeply religious singing. When Vincent van Gogh wanted to devote his life to preaching and evangelization, he set out for the Borinage in Belgium where, besides Catholicism, many Protestant organizations flourish, where even religious healers such as Antoine le Guérisseur found large and enthusiastic audiences.

Mining has been carried on in Belgium for centuries, in Walloonia, the southern part of the country. Up to the end of the eighteenth century coal was extracted from the flanks of the hills, but at present miners go down sixteen hundred yards and even more. Since 1914 mines have developed in Limburg under conditions far different from and better than those in the south.

The mines have transformed the lovely soft-rolling countryside of Hainaut and Liége into an industrial inferno, an enormous Pittsburgh. In daytime a thick layer of coal dust sifts down on the poor meadows, on the slate-

covered roofs, everywhere. Huge mounds of slag rise up
in the neighborhood of every colliery, and in time of stress
people are seen trying to glean the good coal out of the
refuse of the mines which has been piling up for decades.
When rains pour down on this region, scarcely any place
on earth except the English mining districts and parts of
Pennsylvania can be more depressing. At night high
flames from the blast furnaces lick the sky and give the
landscape a terrifying beauty. But even amid this desolation and aridity some villages are spared. They remain as
lovely as those in the Ardennes or in Flanders.

Mines are extremely numerous in Belgium. Most of
them are rich, but as a rule the seams are thin, some being
no more than a yard in height, and very often the miners
have to lie flat on the ground in order to hack into the
soft coal. Their great, implacable enemy is "firedamp,"
tremendous explosions of which may be provoked by the
slightest spark. It is odorless, tasteless and colorless, and
creeps up to the roof of the low tunnels. In olden days the
miners used to take down canaries which lost consciousness when the *grisou* gas was present. Nowadays a special
contraption on top of their individual lamps warns them.
But still every year about two hundred workers fall victims to this horrible menace. On those occasions the people of Walloonia show their mettle. Invariably they prove
to be "heroes without bravado and men with a big heart."
Rescue squads are always more numerous than required.
Periodically the Belgian magazines used to reproduce pictures of these brave men with grim, set faces going down
into the pits to help their comrades, while at the gates of
the colliery anxious women and children stood waiting for
news of the victims.

The Borinage and the Liége districts were indeed tragic regions but, strangely enough, none of the people ever seemed to want to leave. Even when some mines gave out and when other jobs awaited the workers, they stuck to the villages where their fathers had worked rather than move ten or twenty miles from their own homes.

The mining industry shaped the bodies and souls of these people and made them one of the most characteristic groups among the Belgians. Being used to darkness, they enjoyed light and leisure the more. Sitting on their haunches on their doorsteps, looking with loving care at the Jupiter's beard that hung from the roofs of their small houses, on Sundays they waited anxiously for their racing pigeons to dive through the clouds. In the quiet of the Sunday morning, in every village there was sure to be a melomaniac rehearsing with clumsy energy the tuba score of some languorous but showy band piece. In the afternoon people were wont to shoot arrows or play *crosse,* a simplified kind of golf in which only one club is used, or they enjoyed their favorite form of handball, a swift, energetic pastime, a variation on the venerable *jeu de paume.*

Several Belgian sovereigns since the Middle Ages have complained about the stubbornness of the Flemings, but the Walloons call themselves the *tiesses di hoye*—coalheads, and they don't mean soft coal. Together with the Flemish textile workers they were in the front line of the Belgian proletariat when in the eighties they had to fight for the right to unionize or to strike. In 1886 a number of them died as victims of the vain efforts of a shortsighted regime to curtail their march toward liberty and human dignity. Since then Socialism has found its most fervent advocates among the miners of Charleroi and Liége.

When the Germans took over in 1940, of course they wanted coal mining to go on as usual. They wanted practically everything to go on as usual as long as it went their way. Very soon the Belgians found out that although there was an abundance of coal in the country they could get very little of it for their homes, in fact too little to provide them with sufficient heat. They knew that the reason was quite simple: as in every other domain, the Germans were eating the cake and leaving the crumbs for the population. The Quisling press published a study of the coal situation which gives a good picture of the policy followed by the miners to counteract the German technique of looting. This study throws interesting light on what happened in the mines after 1940. In 1939, the total production of coal was 29,844,000 tons; in 1942 it lost 17 per cent and had gone down to 24,928,000 tons. Production, of course, depends on three factors: the number of days of extraction, the number of miners at work, and the daily output of the average miner.

There were in 1939, 141,906 miners; there are now 147,114 of them, including a number of Soviet prisoners. The Quisling press wonders how, with such an increase in the number of workers, the miners actually at work are less numerous than before. Before the war, the proportion between the number of days of leisure and work days was 7½ per cent; now it is 13.7 per cent, and in April, 1944, it went up to 15 per cent. This proves, the Nazi press says, that the management of the coal mines does not care very much about the reasons for the miners' absence, for out of a total of 532,000 days of absence, more than 100,000 days were totally unjustified.

How about the output of the mines? In 1939 a miner

produced 352 pounds per day, but in 1942 he had lost 20 per cent and his output was down to 281 pounds. Of course, decreased physical stamina influences his work, but the Germans have taken all kinds of measures to encourage the miners, giving them better and more food than the other workers so as to maintain their standard of production.

The Quisling press, however, attributes the diminution of production to the mental state of the mine owners and of the miners. The reason for the lack of coal is patriotism. The Anglophile directors of the Belgian coal mines told their workers: "The Germans take all the coal. Therefore the slogan of patriotic miners should be: 'Don't work too much; pretend to work and keep up appearances. Do not be zealous. Do not sabotage openly.'"

In fact, while the production has gone down by 5,000,-000 tons, the number of days of extraction has gone up since 1939 from 285 to 314. The Nazis underline the fact that through this patriotic action every Belgian has been deprived of half a ton of coal; but, they say, "One is forced to realize that the Germans have not suffered from the results of this deficit. Even if production should go down further, there always would be enough coal for the requirements of Germany." One could scarcely ask for a clearer avowal of German looting.

The underground movement took action to remedy the scarcity of coal in Belgian homes. The Nazi press went as far as to say that pillage of coal cars in railroad stations and yards constituted an industry, a commercial enterprise. This did not refer to isolated action by individual marauders, but to operations of real magnitude, undertaken by organized bands for the purpose of robbing coal cars.

These bands had their chiefs, their assembly points, and
their coal yards. Moreover, whole cars were regularly
stolen from the Belgian industry, said one enemy newspaper, which went on in these terms:

> But this reprehensible activity is not enough for these people,
> for if by chance the coal gives out, then they begin on the coal-
> fields themselves. Thus in the mine works in the central region,
> the mere thefts of electric motors no longer amount to anything
> and the marauders have even succeeded in getting away with an
> electric welding machine belonging to a coal-mining company in
> the central basin and worth more than 60,000 francs.

Thanks to the Germans, "in many drawing rooms in
Belgium the stove has become a merely decorative piece of
furniture," but one could not expect the descendants of
the workers who died in 1886 in the defense of their human rights to take all this sitting down. An heroic but
calm conception of life and death was their privilege in
time of peace; no wonder that under a regime of tyranny
and oppression they took matters in their own hands.

4.—*The Bells Are Silent*

DURING THE MIDDLE AGES THERE WAS SCARCELY A MO-
ment of a man's life when the church failed to tell him
that he was only a pilgrim on this earth, a passer-by on
the highway to eternity. The salutations he exchanged

with his fellow citizens recalled God's vigilance over him; when he ate or drank he thanked the Lord who provided food and wine; when he made a deed or opened his business ledger he invoked God's help and mercy. In Antwerp the Exchange did not open before solemn mass had been said with the financiers and the boys of the curb present, and the presses of the great printer Plantin did not print a word of the polyglot Bible if early in the morning the scholars who translated the Good Book, the proofreaders, and even the foremen of the composing room had not attended divine service.

And then there were the bells in the hundreds of churches and chapels. At daybreak they called people to church, they woke up the city. In every quarter of town they broke through the moist night air, answering each other, the silver tones dripping down on the pointed gables, echoing through the narrow streets, lingering in every cozy courtyard. From then on till dark they solemnly counted the hours, the half-hours, the quarters—even every seven minutes they rang out, to tell the people in a hundred different ways that life is short and should be devoted to the Lord's service. There was no escape from this warning, no hiding place for those who wanted to contradict or to evade that continuously repeated assertion of our metaphysical bondage. Even as Adam could not escape the Lord's voice in the thickets of Eden's garden, so the man of the Middle Ages who wanted to follow his earthly inclinations and passions found it impossible to avoid the steady admonition of the volley of bells over his town.

Bells were used not only for religious purposes. The civil authorities needed them too. They hung them in belfries, high up, so that when enemies approached the city the alarm bell would ring out over the whole town. They gave them impressive names; the one in Antwerp was called *Orida,* for it was tolled only in dire need when a real menace threatened the commonwealth. In other places they gave them proud names like *Roeland* in Ghent, which carried the inscription: "Bell Roeland is my name —When I ring it is for fire—When I chime it is for victory—in Flanders."

But besides all the bells, there were the chimes. The civic pride of the community, its *joie de vivre,* had to find an expression independent of the church: in many places where there was a belfry there was a carillon; in others the carillon was installed in the church spire. Belgium, especially Flanders, was a land of chimes. Even the smaller towns could afford one in the days of their grandeur and on festive occasions let the bells ring over the city.

Most of the church bells and carillons of the Middle Ages existed for centuries in Belgium and in the north of France and in Holland. The art of the *carillonneur* was in high esteem. In summertime bell concerts were organized in the big towns and young people sat on the café terraces or in the parks, holding hands and listening to the tunes that dripped down from the cloudy sky. It was an old-fashioned pleasure, like the enjoyment derived from the airs of a music box, but it linked people intimately with the past, and made them proud of their faded glories.

In the past the Belgians were great masters in the art of the chime. To revive that art they established a school, the only one in the world, for carillon players, and most Americans who play the chimes have studied under the guidance of that great virtuoso Jef Denijn, whose pupil,

Kamiel Lefévere, is the bell master at The Riverside Church in New York.

Some time ago when the Germans decided that they needed the Belgian bells, they encountered a resistance which they did not in the least expect and which they considered stupid. These professional "sentimentalists" at times understand little about the soul of things. They are most of the time like that scholarly character of whom James Thurber says: "He doesn't know anything except facts." For them the bronze of the bells had no more moral significance than the iron of the fences which they requisitioned, but the Belgian population felt otherwise. For them the requisitioning of the church and belfry bells was little less outrageous than the abduction of hundreds of thousands of men and women to industrial slavery in Germany.

The church authorities protested against the measure, the Pope intervened without success, and in some parishes the priests, in order to enhance with due dramatic solemnity the cardinal's protest, had the bells ringing all the time while they read the pastoral letter. All over Belgium the order was given to refuse any collaboration whatsoever in the execution of the German requisition. The Nazis, attempting to make this seizure seem less arbitrary, proclaimed that they would spare the bells which had historical value, but in a country where nearly every building of importance is an historical monument, that distinction had no reasonable basis. When German officers called on Mgr. Delmotte, bishop of martyred Tournai, and asked him to name the bells of historical importance, he replied, "They may be historical monuments or not, your crime remains the same. I refuse to say anything." In proud Liége the bishop, Mgr. Kerkhofs, refused to hand over the keys of the cathedral tower. In dozens of cities and villages the Nazis met the same reception—silent and dignified resistance.

In smaller towns when the contractors were ready to execute the German order, the population took matters into their own hands. In several places when the workmen assigned to take away the bells appeared, someone sounded the alarm to warn the inhabitants of the town to be present when the bells were stolen. That happened in Beringen, in Brugge (Bruges), in Ghent, as well as in Moll and in Visé. In Liége the workmen did their job under a hail of stones at the St. Antoine church, and German gendarmes had to intervene. When the bells were down, people inscribed huge V's on them and when the trucks left, the people of Liége sang the national anthem in protest. In Mons and Namur the bells were photographed and the pictures sold for the benefit of a fund to replace the stolen bells after the war.

At Hollogne the priest refused to give up the keys of the church and the Germans had to force the door. When the bell had been brought down, the priest covered it with a tricolor flag. At this signal the bell was immediately covered with flowers brought by numerous demonstrators. When the bell was lifted onto the truck, the flowers were again placed on the bell and as the truck drove away, the crowd sang "La Brabançonne" and some the "Internationale."

In several instances the underground movement by bold strokes succeeded in frustrating the Germans in their requisitioning job. Bells had been taken down to be sent to

Germany; at night patriots drove up to the churches and carried the bells away to safe hiding places.

The German commander in Belgium wanted 3,000 tons of bronze immediately. Of the 3,253 churches, 1,326 had already been despoiled. Belgium's singing towers are silent. The Fuehrer needed the bronze of its bells to combat the Allies, to fight the Belgian airmen in the skies, the Belgian seamen in the North Sea. He needed them to fight the Belgian spirit.

For many centuries these bells have rung out over the Flemish and Walloon towns, proclaiming the Belgians' belief in spiritual values and their unconquerable civic pride. Brute force has taken away the symbol, but the belief and the pride remain. The Germans may break the metal of their bells; they will never break the mettle of their souls.

5.—*The Golden River Enslaved*

THROUGH FLANDERS FIELDS FLOWS THE RIVER LEIE. (Pronounce it Ly-e, or if you want to translate it into French, make it Lys.) It is a peaceful provincial stream which has nothing to compete with the Mississippi or the Nile, or even with the Rhine or the Moldau. It is just a congenial little Flemish river, which is born in northern France and ends its life by merging with the better-known and more pretentious Scheldt, in the old city of Ghent where the United States once made a peace treaty with Great Britain. Geographically that is all there is about the Leie.

It doesn't cascade down high rocks. It doesn't flow through underground grottoes. It doesn't spread out into spacious romantic lakes. It just keeps flowing along, winding a sinuous route through the flat Flanders region. The only peculiarity of its course is that it is as tortuous as an editorial by Mr. Goebbels. It takes its time.

The good people of Ghent use it for excursion purposes. In summertime, in order to escape the combined gloom of their belfry, their medieval castles and unfinished Gothic churches, and also to get away from the drabness of their industrial slums, they embark upon flimsy boats, most of the time in mixed groups. Moving under their own power or propelled by clumsily handled oars, these boats puff and splash their way from Ghent to the countryside. Inevitably after a few hundred yards these groups start to sing. In the beginning it is only shouting and vocal horseplay (hoarse as well), but soon enough one of the girls—they are indispensable on these nautical excursions—succeeds in impressing the company with her voice and then real singing gets under way. It is all about the Leie; they call it the Golden River, they exalt it above the Danube and the Jordan with a slightly irritating but altogether charming local absolutism. From what they sing and say one would gather the impression that their provincial navigations compare favorably with Cleopatra's stately travels down the Nile. They certainly think a lot of the Leie over there.

Since the landscape is as flat as a restaurant pancake, all

the singers can see is the tall reeds along the stream, the knotty willow trees, and a few cows who dare to come close to the water. On the wooden bridges over the river there always sits a slightly adenoidal fisherman, and in the distance one sees the steep spires of the many rural churches.

The trip is always interrupted for a stop in one of the many small "eateries" along the river where eels are served, for the Belgians, like all Europeans, are very fond of these fish. They add butter, parsley and half a dozen other herbs, and proclaim the result a delicacy. You can trust them on that.

Later on, the excursionists re-embark. Without exception the motor gives out and is eventually coaxed back into action; the rowers are tired and the boats zigzag over the nearly motionless water. One more bend and the landscape widens; it hollows out smoothly like a shallow cup; it becomes increasingly beautiful. But invariably the boats turn around. Chinese lanterns are lighted. The girls take out their handkerchiefs in protest. The excursion has reached the frontier of the flax country, and only those who are engaged in the trade can stand its smell. All others have to retreat. For once the people of Ghent give up and go back home. From then on the Leie is on her own. From there on she is entirely devoted to the glory of the Kortrijk (kor-trek) region, to flax and linen.

From time immemorial the growing of flax has been one of the principal activities of Flanders. In the land of Kortrijk more than 50,000 workers are still engaged in it. They grow flax in the low marshes along the river, which overflows periodically and covers a wide stretch of land on both sides. They weed it, faces to the wind, moving on their hands and knees, carefully extirpating all the parasitic plants which spring up so generously from a damp and rich soil. Later on, when the blue bolls have matured, they pull out the whole plant, bundle it into sheaves and let it dry. For months the sheaves stand in the fields, awaiting further processing. The next treatment comes a year later. It is the most important one, for it determines the whiteness of the linen which will be made from the flax fibers. To put it plainly, it is called "rotting," but polite people say "retting." The dried flax is put into shallow trays and sunk in the river Leie to rot. There is no more to it except that one has to know when the process of decomposition is completed, for one can easily overdo it and thus spoil the product. But otherwise the river does all the work; the only thing the people have to do is to stand the rather objectionable smell.

In no other place in the world has there been found a water that helps so much to achieve the whiteness of the flax fibers as the Leie does. The Russian flax growers used to send their Archangel flax to Belgium to have it retted in the Leie waters, and when practically nobody else in Belgium was in contact with Russia, those good provincial burghers of Kortrijk were regularly making long-distance calls to their Soviet customers. Most of the "Irish" linen is originally Belgian, although international snobbism prevents it from being labeled as such, but well-informed people know that the Kortrijk flax and linen is "of unapproached excellence."

For ages the women of the Low Countries have prized this whitest of linen. They used to keep their immaculate table services in huge carved cupboards, and it was with solemn pride that they opened these treasure chests, which gave off a faint lavender smell. Linen and flax were used as terms of poetical comparison: children were "flaxen-haired," and linen was almost a synonym for purity. The greatest of all Flemish novels has as its theme the flax harvest. Flax brought riches to the fertile land of Kortrijk, and the people who knew they owed it to the Leie called it a "golden river."

When the Germans occupied Belgium, they took stock of the reserves of textiles. They did more: they took the stock and carried it away. The textile industry, which for many centuries has been *the* typical Flemish occupation, was immediately reduced to less than 30 per cent of its prewar output. This was due not only to the abduction of a great number of textile workers to slave labor in the Reich, or to the ravages the war had wrought in Flanders, but most of all to the fact that there was little sense in producing textiles likely to be considered luxuries at the time, or flax tow which the Germans could put to good use. Linen yarn was exported to a value of $3,000,000 a year, and more than $5,000,000 worth of luxury fabrics used to leave the country each year before the invasion.

Menaced by starvation, the farmers of the region quite naturally abandoned the traditional growing of flax for the cultivation of oats and potatoes, which they needed far more. There at least they had a chance to get their share, for the Germans were taking away as much as 85 per cent of the flax production. The New Order found out about this situation and, of course, intervened right at the moment flax cultivation was going to collapse almost entirely.

The German *Verordnungsblatt* of the military administration decided that "in order to ensure the growing of compulsory flax quotas, any infringements of regulations will be punished. Penalties will also be incurred by any persons inciting others to infringe this order and fail to cultivate flax." The decree foresaw that the flax growers would have some difficulty in obtaining the necessary flaxseed. Elaborate instructions were given to them as to where to apply for the seed.

Some time ago the Germans told the Belgian farmers they ought to cultivate more rapeseed. They tried to induce them to do so by promising them that part of the production would result in an increase of the fat rations. The Belgian peasants, knowing that rape is a poison for their soil, and well-informed about the real intentions of the Germans, refused to obey the orders. Later on the underground movement took the matter in hand. Colza fields were burned, barns where the harvest was stored were pillaged. In Flanders the same policy was applied to some flax fields. The patriots won the battle of the flax as they won the battle of the colza.

6.—*No More Wings Over Belgium*

IF WE BELIEVE THE "ENCYCLOPAEDIA BRITANNICA"—AND who would dare question the authority of such an institution?—"Belgium may be considered as *par excellence* the home of the pigeon-racing sport." The fact that the Britannica had to resort to a foreign tongue to make herself clear shows that she is in earnest and that she has abundant proofs for her statement.

Believe it or not—after all, who cares?—but there are as many pigeons in Belgium as there are inhabitants, and they multiply faster. More than eight million Belgians, more than eight million pigeons, and many more to come.

How did this come about? Because the Belgians really love them. Consider the attitude of other countries toward the gentle dove! There is no reason to burden the Germans with more sins than they have committed; it is, however, a fact that the two most important books, scholarly volumes of course, which they published on the subject treat the pigeon from the utilitarian and military standpoint. One is called: *Die Brieftaube in der Kriegskunst, The Carrier Pigeon in Warfare,* the other: *Anzucht, Pflege und Dressur der Brieftaube, Raising, Breeding and Training the Carrier Pigeon.* They also called their World War airplanes *Tauben* or pigeons, an improper and deceptive name. It was a minor although characteristic sin.

Among the most celebrated of another group of Axis pigeons were those of San Marco in Venice. In summer they suffered from acute indigestion, being overfed by American schoolteachers. The Italians even came to depend on that.

Therefore it is all the more discouraging to learn that the last aboriginal American pigeon—you shall be spared the Latin name—died a solitary death in Cincinnati in 1914. All the familiar parasites of St. Patrick's church are just plain immigrants like you and me.

In Belgium pigeons are loved for three reasons: they

may be prized for their beauty, they may be appreciated for their tastiness when cooked, and finally they may be appraised for their ability to make money.

The Belgians had all kinds of ornamental doves: white turtledoves with queer red round eyes, lovely and slightly ridiculous birds which had nothing to do but to float around, to sit and look as immaculate as a bride's veil, to coo and to woo—in short, to live a life of comfort and beauty everyone secretly envied. Occasionally these de luxe birds would be put in a cage and sent to a show and then the cooing would be done by the enthusiastic visitors of the show and by the fond owners.

The pigeon in Belgium was the poor man's chicken and the rich man's delight. Every convalescent was entitled to a tender young pigeon for his first real meal, the initial step on the road to readaptation to the heavy meat diet of the land. When the old Flemish painters represent the Land of Plenty, fried pigeons descend into the mouths of loafers who object to moving their limbs even to feed themselves. A fried pigeon was a democratic treat, at the disposal of the poor as well as of the rich.

Last but not least, the pigeon was valued as a money earner. We all, to different degrees however, have the homing instinct. Ulysses takes nine years to come home from Troy, but anyway he comes home. Certain husbands leave their homes at night to buy cigarettes at the corner drugstore. They may come back after five years and simply say, "They were out of Camels," but back they come! Lassies come home in technicolor; eels travel thousands of miles to die in their native abode in the Sargasso Sea, but nature's masterpiece of the homing instinct is the pigeon. This the Belgians have understood the best of all people, and being practical-minded, they have exploited it with consistency and adroitness.

Since 1820 they have organized long-distance flying for pigeons. The first race was between Liége and Paris (90 miles). Then pigeons were sent to London, and gradually the racing distances were increased. They went to Rome (730 miles) and Barcelona (660 miles), to Ajaccio (630 miles) and even to Algiers (950 miles). Weather permitting, they traveled fast, doing as much as 70 miles an hour, but they traveled intelligently: they took 30 hours in a storm for a flight which took them three hours in fair weather. They stopped at night. Sometimes hawks attacked them and sometimes they hurt themselves on telephone wires.

By careful selection and interbreeding the Belgians succeeded in producing a specimen of streamlined efficiency and high speed, the height of perfection in carrier pigeons, which is known all over the continent as the "Antwerp carrier pigeon." When telephone booths were crowded, these pigeons were used by some newspapers to dispatch race results.

The approximately 400,000 race-pigeon owners were so fond of their favorites that their innocent game evoked the suspicion of the economists, who for once turned to moralizing about the situation. They found out in 1930 that the Belgians spent about $20,000,000 per year on tobacco, $15,000,000 on alcohol, $10,000,000 on shows, but also $5,000,000 on pigeons. They calculated that the upkeep of a pigeon costs about $1.10 a year, and they found pigeon-racing to be a "burdensome though soothing" kind of sport.

But if some people care about what moralists say, who

cares about the warnings of economists who point an in-dignant finger at an altogether harmless pastime which might cost a few dollars a year but which might also bring a good reward in prizes or even riches to the owner of some extraordinarily speedy specimen of the "Antwerp carrier pigeon"?

Not all the owners of pigeons wanted to make money on the homing instinct of their birds; many kept them mostly for pleasure. In every Belgian village one could find people who would sit for hours observing the antics of some strutting pigeon wooing an ever-evading but never completely escaping mate. Through analogy one could develop quite a philosophy of marital relations from these homelike scenes. The Spaniards say that an orchard with a pigeon house is an earthly paradise. They must have learned that in Flanders, which they occupied for such a long time.

This is war, and not even the billing dove, the patient dove, the gentle dove—whatever it has been called by the poets who must know—has escaped its horrors. During the siege of Paris in 1870 the French used pigeons to mail their messages out of the city, but the Germans trained hawks to intercept these swift messengers. In the First World War more than 120,000 pigeons were used by the German army alone. In the present war a great number of pigeons have been used by all the armies, and one of the first ordinances the Germans issued after occupying a town was directed toward obtaining a complete list of all the pigeons in the community. In several cases, suspecting the owners of some dark design, they simply pointed their machine guns at the pigeon cotes and killed the birds. A great number of them died in this way during the invasion and afterward.

The German military commander of Belgium and northern France prohibited the keeping of any pigeons in the whole coastal region of Belgium, in Brussels, Mons, and Liége—in virtually four-fifths of the Belgian territory. The identification rings the birds wear had to be surrendered to the local mayors so as to permit a checkup when birds were killed or died.

Thus the Germans succeeded in taking the birds out of the sky. It was a great new triumph for the National Socialist idea. In a new domain "order" was established. Most of the Belgian doves bled to death. Their owners preferred to kill them rather than to have them serve the enemy and his foul purposes. The same feeling which leads Anglo-Saxon people to lavish such an astonishing amount of sentimental affection on dogs and horses inspires the Belgians toward their pigeons. For many of them this stab at the gentle dove was a terrible shock. One may feel that this is a ridiculously exaggerated pity, but how can one forget that the first time the dove appears in history it was a symbol of peace, and that since then when it showed itself in the heavens, when it circled around a rural church spire, or lighted on an old moss-covered wall, it was always the sign that idyllic and peaceful conditions prevailed and that men had found some way of living together without flying at each other's throats?

That familiar sight was seen no more; the doves had gone from the Belgian skies. For a time no other bird flew above the rich loam of the Belgian earth and over the age-old gables of the cities but the German eagle. But this latter will shortly lose its last plumes and totter earthward. You may be sure that out of nowhere, at that moment, thousands of doves, eternal symbols of peace and victory, will soar into the cloudy skies of a free Belgium.

7.—*The Battle of the Press*

IN "THE MOON IS DOWN," ONE OF MR. STEINBECK'S characters expressed very aptly the position of the occupying authorities in a Nazi-conquered country which refuses to admit defeat. In despair, one of the German officers, harassed by the constant nagging and opposition of the populace, says: "The flies have conquered the fly paper." Belgium provides a remarkable illustration of this technique.

When the Germans marched into Belgium, in May, 1940, the first thing they did was to throttle the freedom of the press. Up to that day, Belgian newspapers had been in the habit of saying whatever came into their minds; now they were going to print what was in Mr. Hitler's mind. Of course, the Nazis told the Belgians that their newspapers before the invasion were no good. In fact, opinions may have differed on that point: some people felt that the Belgian press was a marvelous ensemble, others thought that they had just the press they deserved, but anyway the Belgians had their own press which fulfilled their essential requirements in that field and reflected both the qualities and weaknesses of the national character. It was not influenced by foreign money and, during the "phony war," it proved abundantly that it stood only for Belgian interests and was not afraid to proclaim its profound sympathy for the Allied cause. There were, however, two exceptions: one Flemish and one French newspaper, which had in the last few years been defending Fascist ideas and which were at the beck and call of Hitler and Mussolini, sided violently with the Axis. The first one, *Volk en Staat (The People and the State)*, was the organ of the Flemish nationalist movement, which had adopted not only the basic ideas of the Nazi program, but which also used the despicable antics of Nazi journalism and polemics. On the other hand, there was the French newspaper, *Le Pays Réel (The Real Country)*, which was the organ of the Rexist (Fascist) leader Léon Degrelle who, by the spectacular vulgarity of his political campaigns attained a fame entirely disproportionate to his intelligence and talent.

As soon as the German Command settled down in Belgium the people who had always been friendly to the Germans hoped to be given the direction of public affairs. As faithful servants of the Nazi regime they counted on being privileged to enlighten the Belgian public. Their first disillusionment—one in a long series—came when the Germans decreed that not only the two Fascist newspapers which for so long had deserved a reward, but also all the other newspapers of normal times, should be placed on a firm footing. The Nazis' main preoccupation was to have the Belgian scene look as normal as possible. Nothing was to be changed in the Belgian press except the spirit. The editors of the Belgian newspapers, except those of the two Fascist newssheets, refused to go on publishing their journals under German control and influence. Practically all of them were dismissed and dispossessed of their presses and premises. Some of them who had been especially forceful in their resistance were sent to jail. The editor of a widely read Antwerp newspaper, who had been a prisoner of the Germans during the last war, was sent once more to a concentration camp, where he died. In the southern part of the country, the editor of a Liége newspaper, who presided over the Belgian Press Association, was treated in the same way, and died shortly after being released from prison. The director of the Belgian News Agency suffered the same fate.

The newspapers were handed over by the Nazis to a number of doubtful characters of poor literary abilities and even poorer professional morals. They became mere Nazi propaganda sheets, receiving their directives and instructions every day from the German Propaganda *Staffel*. The Belgian public lost interest in these papers, and patriots boycotted them, refusing to buy them or even to advertise in them. But still a number of people had to subscribe for purely economic or social reasons. When the Nazis found out about the reluctance of the Belgian public, they looked for a means of forcing them to buy the Quisling newspapers. They achieved their aim by publishing exclusive information about the food supply, the rations, and other vital matters in the Quisling press. Even so, circulation was very small compared to prewar figures.

In an attack on a Quisling editor one of the Belgian underground newspapers defined very well the limited significance and effect the Quisling press had on the public. "You cannot be accused of influencing public opinion. Nine-tenths of the readers of your paper read nothing but news about the food supply, the stock exchange, sports, births, deaths and marriages. The remaining tenth read your articles not because they attach any particular value to them, but in order to pick out material for charges they will bring against you one day."

From time to time the Quisling press ventured to express slight criticism of some insignificant detail of the policy of the occupying authorities. To counteract such impertinences the Germans had their own German newspaper, the *Brüsseler Zeitung,* which published every day the Nazi gospel truth, and which, in order to give the Belgian public the impression that the Quisling press had a certain freedom, once in a while delivered editorial spankings to the editors of the collaborationist organs.

In the meantime the two hundred newspapers of the underground most effectively combated the poisonous effect the Quisling press might have among the population. As the resistance got better organized a more aggressive policy was followed. Not only did the patriots advise people not to buy those Quisling papers, unless they were absolutely indispensable, but they decided to discourage the subscribers of the two most rabidly collaborationist papers. This was easier in small communities than in big towns, and soon the *Pays Réel* was writing that it was not safe any more for their subscribers to read their paper, that especially in small villages everybody was informed of the names of the Nazi sympathizers who read their paper regularly, and that those people were ostracized by their neighbors, thus suffering injury not only in their social relations but also in their business interests.

As things developed, the relations between the protected Nazi press and the hunted underground press developed as follows. On the one hand there existed about twenty newspapers, provided with all the paper they wanted, using the best presses in Belgium, having at their disposal not only the good will and the protection of the Germans but also trucks and railroad facilities for distribution, together with the means of effectively forcing people to buy their journals, staffed by well fed and highly paid traitors. On the other hand there were two hundred small secret papers, which had to get their paper at high cost and by secret means, which had to be printed underground, which patriots distributed at the risk of their lives; they were written, composed and printed by people who were underfed, lacking heat and clothing—most of them probably old men, all the able-bodied men having been shipped out of Belgium as slave laborers to Germany —all of them working under the constant menace of the Nazi ordinances, which condemned them to death or to prison.

Some timorous people, seeing the tremendous sacrifices and dangers to which the editors, printers, and distributors of the underground press freely consented, at one time asked whether it was really worth while to take all those risks in order to distribute small newspapers which, after all, as they felt, could not accomplish a great deal. The underground press answered these hesitations by saying that no price was to be esteemed too high to encourage and keep up the national spirit and that in the end events would prove that the editors of the underground press were right. What has happened in the last few months has proved their point.

Most of the Quisling editors had by this time understood that the Germans had lost the war and, consequently, that their game was up. They wanted to save their lives. Some of them had even gone so far as to provoke the Nazis in order to get themselves arrested and by so doing to regain some kind of patriotic virginity, which, in their calculations at least, would absolve them from Belgian justice after the liberation of the country. The Nazi editor of the principal Belgian newspaper *Le Soir* called his staff together in November, 1943, and told them in a long speech, which he wanted them to repeat outside the office: "We have collaborated with the Germans because we thought they were going to win the war. We made a mistake. They are losing it. Furthermore, the Germans are not what we thought them to be. They are stupid; they will never understand other countries. They promised to liberate 20,000 Belgian prisoners of war; they did not keep their promise. In conclusion, they are no good." According to his expectations, the traitor who made this speech was arrested by the Germans, but so great was their scorn for him that after a few days, knowing that he had become useless to them, that he was hated by his countrymen and could no longer be an instrument of their policy, they released him.

A little later the organ of the Rexist (Fascist) Party made an even more sensational confession. An editorial in that paper said: "Lost in the hostile, crafty mass of the population, overwhelmed with rumors, wading through the shameful mire which is daily submerging our com-

rades and institutions, we are enveloped in dense mists."
After this brief description of the situation of the Quisling
party, the editorial goes on complaining about the fact
that the party cannot "come together regularly and hold
periodic regional meetings. Times have changed." The
editor concludes that only one asset has remained intact—
their newspaper—but even that is menaced. The editors
and subscribers are in danger of their lives, surrounded by
patriots who resort to the most violent sabotage, so that
being a subscriber to the *Pays Réel* is coming very close to
heroism, but, says the editor: "We are no cowards and we
shall hold our ground proudly and full of courage."

However, it is well known that courage does not ex-
clude prudence, and it must be said that the conclusion to
which the few Fascists in Belgium came was to exercise
extreme caution. The masters of the political situation in
Belgium had no other solution to offer to their followers
than to resort to an extraordinary measure. They worded
it as follows: "In certain cases our activity might gain by
becoming somewhat less spectacular and more discreet.
We need our militants too badly to expose them so light-
heartedly to the knights of the mask and tommy gun
[This text refers to the patriotic saboteurs]. At the moment we are busy drawing up a new system of distribution
which will enable our readers to elude undesirable observers. We will answer stealth with stealth. If necessary the
Pays Réel will go underground, but it will get through
under the very noses of Stalin and his gang. This will only
add spice to our activities. In defiance of threats and ter-
rorism our subscriptions must be maintained at our present level. In fact, we have not given up hope. We must
win the battle of our press."

The Nazi sheets, according to their own confession, were driven out of circulation by the patriotic press. The traitors anxiously prepared their alibis to present to the Belgian courts. The battle of the Belgian press was already decided.

The time has come when the Belgian people are chasing their enemies around the walls of Festung Europa as Achilles chased the swift-footed Hector three times around the high-walled city of Troy. Everybody knows the end of that combat and how Hector was left lying on the shore to be devoured by dogs and vultures. It is highly improbable that Mr. Hitler, like another Priam, will come out of his castle to claim their corpses.

8.—*The Underground Speaks*

AMONG THE ONE HUNDRED AND NINETY UNDERGROUND newspapers which were circulated in occupied Belgium, *La Libre Belgique* was certainly the most famous and the most widely read. Its history dates back to the First World War. At that time there was no radio, and foreign newspapers were prohibited in Belgium. Only the Dutch newspapers managed to get in from time to time, but they were usually heavily censored by the Germans, and people were forced to depend almost entirely on rumors as far as news of the Allies was concerned. Before long, the strain of consistently reading the German communiqués in reverse began to tell on the Belgian people, and their morale began to be badly in need of a boost. The underground press provided this stimulus by giving reliable Allied information about the war and acting at the same time as the spokesman of patriotic feeling. *La Libre Belgique* acquitted itself of its task with remarkable success. Its journalistic standards were high, and its editorial policy was beyond reproach from the national standpoint. Politics were shelved for the duration, and no partisan opinion was allowed to color its writing. The little weekly became a thorn in the side of the Germans and they hunted it from one corner of the country to another. Sometimes they succeeded in seizing and confiscating an issue. More often they arrested writers and printers who they thought were responsible for its publication. But they never succeeded in discovering the real leader of the organization.

Only a few weeks after the occupation of Belgium in 1940, *La Libre Belgique* started its new series under even more difficult conditions than in 1914. The danger was as great, but the times had changed. It was no longer possible for the Germans to prevent Allied news from reaching Belgium. Belgians in exile spoke to their countrymen over the BBC from London. The Germans considered for a while confiscating all radio sets, but they finally abandoned the idea in favor of attempting to influence the Belgians through their own Quisling broadcasts. Although heavy penalties were meted out to those who were caught listening to the BBC, the Germans in their press and public statements admitted that practically every Belgian listened to the London radio. German officials and Quislings broadcast discussions of the Allied news, and even engaged in polemics with the BBC, a procedure which would have been ridiculous had not the Germans realized that the London radio was one of the normal sources of information for the Belgians. But still there was a place for the printed word, a task for it to perform in the interest of the country. *La Libre Belgique* reappeared, and all over Belgium dozens of French and Flemish underground publications sprang up. However, since times had changed, the editors decided to adapt themselves to the new circumstances. The main task of the nation was to sabotage the enemy war effort in every trade, in every industry and in every intellectual activity. Therefore, the underground newspapers devoted themselves systematically to instructing different groups of people on the part they were to play in the general resistance. The peasants had *De Boer* (*The Farmer*) and *Le Bon Combat* (*The Good Fight*), the railway workers had *La Voix du Cheminot* (*The Voice of the Railwayman*), students and professors of the closed University of Brussels read the *Bulletin des Amis de l'Université Libre de Bruxelles*, or *Jeunesse*; other students and professors read *Enseignement* (*Teaching*), and women read *La Voix des Femmes* (*The Women's Voice*).

The publication and the circulation of these newspapers demanded, of course, a considerable amount of energy and a daily renewal of heroism. Apparently some people asked themselves if these sacrifices of brave lives were really worthwhile, and if all that energy could not have been used to a better end. This question was answered by an article in one of these underground newspapers:

Is there any use in a victim's crying helplessly for assistance? Of course there is, even if help does not come immediately. The existence of an underground paper means that nothing will drown the voice of patriotism. It means that in order to oppose a tyrannical and barbarian regime, there are men and women and young people who voluntarily take up an outlaw's life, full of obscure hardships, of secret action, devotion, daring and danger.

The question was also asked as to how large a group of people each of these secret newspapers really reached. *The Voice of the Belgians* answered the question:

During the last eighteen months, more than a quarter of a million papers carrying our name have been circulated throughout the country. Counting four readers for each paper, the total represents quite a wide circulation. If the circulation in the Walloon provinces is proportionately large, the Flemish provinces have not been forgotten, and in certain districts enthusiastic friends translate our articles regularly to a group of patriots who do not understand French at all, or whose knowledge of the language is insufficient. We have several times been asked to provide a Flemish edition for these people—not a second paper; what is wanted is one paper published in each of our two national languages, for both Walloons and Flemings. But as our friends understand very well, circumstances have up to now prevented us from complying with their legitimate request.

On the basis of these figures and other information, it can safely be said that the entire Belgian population was reached by the underground press.

The Voice of the Belgians continued with a discussion of its financial situation and says:

On the day of liberation we shall publish detailed accounts, and it will then be seen that not a centime has been wasted or has remained in the hands of those who received the money. Without waiting for this date, we would like to express our gratitude to all those Belgians who are helping us and to publish for them our

1942 balance sheet. Expenditure amounts to 210,245.35 Belgian francs divided as follows:

Newspaper expenses—161,134.35 francs; grants for patriotic activities—29,513 francs; debts at present not recoverable—19,578 francs.

Receipts amounted to 201,241.20 Belgian francs divided as follows:

Sale of papers (money received by the central fund, after deduction of sums allowed to local committees for their own activities)—76,567.20 francs; supporters' contributions—102,614.-75 francs; advances (no hope of repayment) by members of the staff—22,059.25 francs. This figure would probably alarm the prudent, but we just smile, as it does not represent even a fifth of the 1941 deficit. We are quite convinced that the generosity of patriots will not fail to pay off this deficit and even more.

The honesty and integrity of these editors add to the power of their voice. Upon their shoulders was placed the responsibility of lifting the morale of their people when the difficulties seemed insurmountable and then of transforming a passive resistance into active and open sabotage of every phase of the oppressor's war effort. To these men and to their colleagues in all occupied countries we owe a great debt of gratitude and profound admiration for their courage and unfailing hope in the new world for which they fight.

9.—*Disorder in the New Order*

A GREAT DEAL HAS BEEN SAID ABOUT THAT WONDERFUL
wartime industrial machine which Germany organized and
which, according to legend and popular belief, ran so
smoothly that it transformed even those who operated it
into robots. However, the more we hear about it in detail,
the more apparent it becomes that this marvel of German
ingenuity may occasionally have functioned with a disor-
ganization similar to that sometimes seen in the Allied
war effort. One of the best illustrations of this was the
technic which the Nazis used to requisition labor in Belgium and the way they used their slave manpower in the
Reich.

It is evident that apart from a rough outline of official
policy, individual and local German authorities in the occupied countries usually followed their own inspiration or
fancy. They first approached the big plants, requisitioning
10 or 15 per cent of the personnel; then they went to work
on the smaller businesses. Employers who had just one
worker had him taken away, and those who had no help
at all were often themselves shipped to Germany without
further ado. In a number of towns, the shopkeepers of
certain quarters were sent to Germany, while in other
quarters of the same town they were left alone.

The first step in recruiting was to mail a number of people an order to call at the *Werbestelle,* the recruiting station. The lists were obtained from the local authorities either by brute force or by pressure. Since those lists mentioned only the age and occupation of each man or woman, a great number of people who were unemployable showed up at the recruiting station. When those were sent home, certain people still remained who were not desirable workers for one reason or other. Pupils of technical and professional schools were highly desirable for slave labor, but while in most of the towns they were invariably signed up for deportation, in Mons their recruitment was postponed and in Namur it was halted.

Women as well as men were recruited and the same arbitrary technic was applied to them as to the men—percentage recruiting in the factories, surprise recruiting in restaurants and department stores. Women were also arrested in the streets. In many cases women servants were taken from the houses of their employers.

As for grounds for exemption, there seem to have been some general rules, but every office applied them in its own way and very often these offices changed their minds after a few days. Occasionally they gave in to requests from Belgians, but the leniency didn't last and the regulations were eventually applied with all their original harshness. For a short time women under twenty-four years of age were exempt from forced labor, but after three months the age minimum was lowered to twenty-one. Even girls from fourteen to sixteen years of age have been called to the *Werbestelle.*

In the beginning, the managers of industrial plants who saw themselves being forced to turn over their personnel files to the Germans protested to the recruiting stations. Displeased, the Germans decided that only the National Labor Office could deal with complaints, but the attitude of the NLO officials proved vexing because of their sympathy for the employers, and it was ordered that only individual protests or requests for exemption would be allowed.

Besides obvious physical shortcomings which render people unemployable, the main reason for exemption seemed to be ulcers, cancer, or a loss of forty to fifty per cent of normal vision. Tuberculosis was not a reason for exemption; only when there were other cases in the same family was it considered, and many tuberculosis sufferers who brought their X-ray photographs along to prove their unfitness were shipped to Germany with the comment that the authorities there would find out the extent of their illness.

In order to put up a false front, the Germans asked all men shipped to the Reich to sign a statement, the significance of which they often did not grasp. It stated that they were volunteers. If they signed up to go to Germany "of their free will and in a spirit of solidarity," they immediately received seven hundred and fifty francs as a premium for travel expenses. Those who refused did not receive this premium and other financial advantages for their families. On their workers' cards the Germans put a stamp: *Dienstverplichtet*—forced to work. They received a special pamphlet on the punishment meted out for unwillingness to work or unruliness.

When the workers arrived in the Reich, some were shipped directly to the place where they were to work, others were put together in fields or in hangars where employers could come and look them over. It was an open slave market, the employers picking out the strongest and healthiest men. Very often those not chosen stayed idle for weeks waiting for an employer.

One would suppose that every slave worker would have been used according to his ability. Most of the time this was the case, but the Germans had no scruples whatsoever against breaking the terms of the fake contract they signed and transforming a carpenter into a miner or a watchmaker into a brakeman. Women were as a rule considered to be good for any work, but girls who used to be expert seamstresses were used as charwomen for labor camps. Others were turned into domestics.

Work days were usually ten to twelve hours, but sometimes they were longer. One out of every three Sundays was free. But in spite of this, the Germans constantly complained about the poor output of the Belgian workers. German workers told their foreign colleagues to slow down on the job, with the result that ten hours were required for a job that used to take four.

Usually the workers could buy one meal a day at the factory. In some regions they had a very fair food supply, far better than in Belgium. In other places they were poorly fed, and often asked their families back home to send them packages. They had to pay prohibitive prices for supplementary food, and they found it impossible to send any money home.

Workers were warned by Belgian organizations to take along a number of necessaries—thread, among others— hard to find in Germany. Negligent workers have been known to search for a tin pan for days, and another person who forgot to take along a fork had to put three nails through a piece of wood to help himself out. Worn-out clothes cannot be replaced in Germany; workers had to get replacements from Belgium.

Of course the Gestapo had an eye on all these more or less dissatisfied foreigners. According to a special decree, every worker who committed an act of material or *moral* sabotage could be condemned to prison or to death. Anything might be considered moral sabotage, such as a worker's statement that he had been forced to come to Germany, or a complaint about the food, the lodging or the kind of work. Apparently the only remarks permitted were about the weather.

For relaxation the workers were entirely free. They could go where they wanted. "Organized fun" is, however, not unusual, except occasionally in its form. Groups of Belgian workers, men and women, have been taken to nudist exhibitions where Russian women were forced to appear as performers.

The Belgian clergy is not authorized to organize spiritual assistance for the workers and, on the other hand, the German clergy is not allowed to go into the labor camps, even to administer to the dying. To remedy this situation, Belgian priests have gone to Germany as workers in order to be able to assist their compatriots.

Such is the "wonderful" organization set up by the Germans, a ponderous machine which results in a great waste, which makes millions of people unhappy and miserable, and which results finally in having the best workers of Europe do their job in ten instead of in four hours.

10.—*Eleven Hundred Honest Men*

It is clearly said in the Odyssey that besides his sincere desire to get home, Ulysses wanted "to see many cities of men and learn about their customs and way of life." In other words, he liked to study their institutions, which were the most characteristic expression of their soul and mind.

Only a few decades ago the historians discovered that the essential task of history was not to make a list of more or less intelligent kings and emperors, however influential these individuals were in their country's destiny, but that the real object of their science and research was to depict how people had lived, loved and died through the ages. So they began to study the institutions of man, the framework he put up around his own actions, the conventions which he invented or adapted so that in all major events he might have guidance for his behavior or an instance to which to refer. Soon the study of these institutions revealed far more about the people than the confused history of the amours and battles of sovereigns and tyrants. As the historians advanced in their researches, it became evident that the terms used in different countries, though derived from the same original idea or word, had come to designate institutions entirely different, that if there were "hundreds of kings" on Ulysses' tiny home islands, they bore but slight similarity to Louis XIV and would be better described as chiefs or bosses.

In less important domains the same thing happens on a large scale: that is one of the reasons why Europe and, more especially, Great Britain, although similar in language, have to be explained to Americans. For a judge in Bristol is not what a judge in Columbus is, and a postmaster general in Washington has characteristics quite different from those which distinguish his Belgian or French colleagues.

For a European fresh from the landing pier, one of the most puzzling details about the American cities is the amazing number of notaries public whom he sees advertised in drugstores, cigar counters and hotel lobbies. The first time he happens to come in contact with one of these "officers of the law" his astonishment knows no bounds: he usually is introduced to a girl in her twenties, wearing loud harlequin spectacles and puffing a cigarette from a dangerously long black holder. Few questions are asked. In an imperative voice the young lady orders, "Sign here!" jerks a seal out of a drawer, uses it with determined, silent energy and concludes the operation with the words, "A quarter, please." Some Europeans have spent dollars and dollars to go through that experience again. They simply could not believe their eyes.

In Europe, especially in Belgium and other countries which adopted most of the institutions laid down in the Napoleonic code, as a rule a notary is known as a solemn individual, with an overserious, even slightly morose air.

In olden times, when people wanted to make a deed, sell a house or take out insurance, they appeared before the aldermen of their town, who took down their decisions, kept the record of the transaction, and charged them a fee for the procedure. Almost all we know about everyday life in the cities of the Middle Ages is contained in the registers of the copies of these deeds. Later on, private individuals by special privilege were allowed to officiate as the aldermen—they were the notaries public whose statutory power was definitely established by Napoleon.

The principal characteristic of the notary in Belgium is that he belongs to a closed guild. Only a limited number, about 1100 of them, are allowed to officiate, by governmental order. They are appointed for life, and most of them try to arrange matters so that their sons will inherit their office. If they have no male heirs, they find no difficulty in marrying off their daughters, since the prospective sons-in-law hope to take over their jobs. No land or house can be sold without their assistance. They make wills and marriage contracts, they act as trustees of family funds—in a word, they are indispensable in the most annoying moments of life.

Experience has made them conservative. They know too much. They have seen estates crumble, homes crack up, they have been present when old family feuds flared up and when the "basic social cell" we celebrate so highly turned out to be a nest of entwined vipers. They know that such and such an old maid has willed her whole fortune to the dog and cat hospital, and one day they had to notify a miserable old drunken nitwit that he had inherited a million. They have an orchestra seat at the performance of the human comedy, and enjoy the alternative of being driven crazy by all they know and hear or becoming as impassive as a dreaming Buddha. Most of them decide on the latter. Having found out that a high percentage of people make a mess of their lives, the notaries determine to enjoy life wisely: no one has better wine in Belgium, no one has a better library. Very often no one has better, more or less Voltairian conversation.

Their offices are invariably dusty and dark. One feels that family skeletons are stacked in every corner. The curtains are especially depressing. Waiting in their anterooms, one comes to wonder how such glorious things as life and death and romance should finally be handled in such places by men in stiff starched collars and with absent eyes and icy manners.

They are certainly a far cry from their American colleagues, male and female, as far in appearance as in spirit. They are an element of solidity, order and safety. One trusts them, one respects them, and one sees them—like the dentist—as infrequently as possible.

It took the Nazis three years to find out that these 1100 men believed in their profession, that they were part of the national tradition, that they represented Belgium as much as the judges who went on strike to sabotage German laws, as much as the schoolteachers who refused a Nazi raise.

The Germans have dispossessed thousands of Jewish people in Belgium; they have stolen the belongings of most of those who left the country for political reasons; they take away the property of those they consider saboteurs and enemies of Germany. They have proclaimed that all Belgians residing in the Congo, in England or in the United States of America, all the French, British, Americans or Russians who have property in Belgium, are their enemies, and therefore they have confiscated their possessions. But what good was a house in Brussels or a chateau in Bouillon to Hitler or Goering, since they knew that in a little time they would be driven from this country back to their ruins and their Biergartens? For this reason the Germans wanted to sell the confiscated property and addressed themselves to the notaries public. However, these gentlemen are not fences; their professional honor forbids them to deal in stolen lands and houses. The law says that they are obliged to officiate whenever their offices are required, but the law, feeling that such a paragraph would have been obnoxious, nowhere stipulates that stolen goods are taboo. Everyone knows that except the Germans.

Their hands full of loot, the Nazis asked the notaries to sell it and hand them the money. The notaries, stiffer than ever in their starched shirts, said: No. The Germans insisted, the notaries told them to go where they belonged.

The notaries have a board of discipline: they decide when one of them is no longer worthy of his functions; they punish those of their colleagues who act contrary to the regulations of their profession. They knew that if one of them succumbed to German pressure he would be cast out like a leper by his colleagues.

The Germans could not find one fissure in this wall of resistance. They gave in and decided to leave these eleven hundred brave men alone. On December 21, 1943, the military commander appointed a German Herr Doktor to act as notary public in Belgium. He will be paid on the basis of the German rate and the receipts will go to the German Military Administration.

Of course, the Germans will confiscate and sell Belgian

and Allied property, right and left. Herr Doktor Wester-
mayer will arrange all that. The bootblack of the *Kom-
mandantur* would have done as well, but a Herr Doktor
is more respectable.

In the solemn studies of the Belgian notaries, among
their green filing cabinets and their codes, eleven hundred
men sat and smiled wisely. They knew that brutal conquer-
ors come and go, that violence does not last and, having
seen all the ugly things that crawl at the bottom of the
human heart, they also knew that one gesture of human
decency is enough to wipe out the memory of thousands
of misdeeds. They knew that long after the Nazi thieves
and murderers have left the blessed country of Belgium
and gone into hiding to protect themselves from the aveng-
ing arm of international justice, the memory of the calm
bravery of the Belgian notaries will live on.

11.—*A Flaming Hell*

WHETHER WE ARE CONSCIOUS OF THE FACT OR NOT,
there is something solemn and symbolic in our sitting
down and sharing a meal with others. A certain com-
munion exists in this satisfaction of a basic human need.
It stresses our sameness and a fundamental human achievement when we can partake of food without fighting each
other like animals. The act has a social significance too.

The ancients understood this very well. When the Bible speaks of people eating together, it is always with an almost solemn note, and, in the last song of the *Iliad,* Homer, in his deeply dramatic way, illustrates the point with moving simplicity. He takes his reader's mind away from the horrors of the nine-year-old war of Troy and tells how Priam, King of the beleaguered city, comes to Achilles, leader of the besieging army, to request the surrender of the body of his slain son, Hector. Achilles yields to the father's plea and solemnly arranges the funeral carriage. When everything is prepared, he invites Priam to dinner. Priam sits down and eats with the man who killed his son. Homer explains this astonishing scene by referring to other similar incidents in Greek mythology. Even in the midst of the greatest sorrow, he says, we should go back to this most essential of human needs; we should interrupt our grief to enjoy the goodness of life's simplest privilege. This same Homeric quality was also present more recently, when General Montgomery sat down to a meal in North Africa with a vanquished German general. In the midst of the hatreds which divide us, we should sometimes revert in humility to the essentials of nature which make us all alike.

Civilized people throughout the world have understood this solemn and simple lesson. It took the Nazis to abolish it like so many other things. In a futile and pathetic gesture, Pétain spoke about an armistice "with honor" to be concluded with Hitler. He reverted to the language of chivalry and of gentlemen at the very moment when Hitler was preparing to banish these ideas from the face and the mind of Europe. Honor was a liberalistic scarecrow; the lessons which humanity had learned over a period of two thousand years were to be forgotten. Pétain was the first to learn this—or did he learn it? The Belgians were second. When the battle was over, the victor did indeed sit down to eat with the vanquished; but the gravy went to the victor and the bone to the defeated. There was nothing Homeric about it. The manners were pre-Homeric and dated back to the caveman era.

In peacetime, Belgium used to import about 60 per cent of her wheat from outside Europe. In the course of the last hundred years the food-producing terrain decreased from 2,278,262 to 1,526,846 acres, while the population increased by 78 per cent. To conquer the Belgians was not an easy task but, having conquered them, one was supposed, according to the Hague Convention, to feed them. At least it was supposed that the German administration would have enough decency to let the Belgians retain the produce of their own soil. What actually occurred is common knowledge. Like a horde of locusts, the Nazis descended upon the Flemish farms and the agricultural sections of Walloonia, plundering them in the most shameful fashion. But this preliminary plunder was not enough. A system had to be invented, as time went on, to insure production and enable the Germans to continue this fruitful looting. They therefore organized the Agricultural Corporation which they called "National." In a way it made things easier; every farmer's production record could be checked; but at the same time it provoked such a storm of protest, such stubborn resistance among the peasantry, that to attempt to carry out the corporation policy to the letter became at the same time futile and dangerous.

During the last war, the Belgians had learned to develop smuggling and black-marketing to a fine art. A black market rapidly developed and became a recognized institution among the population. Transgressors brought into court by the Germans heard the judges declare that nobody could remain alive without resorting to the black market.

There were a great number of Nazi troops and an impressive staff of German officials in Belgium. For two years they tried to make the best possible use of their stay in Belgium. They liked to earn a little pocket money. Using their authority and their many means of influencing people without making friends, they organized a highly profitable black market. It became a widespread institution and its existence was repeatedly proved. Apparently the Nazis higher up didn't care very much. The regime tolerated a certain amount of graft as long as it didn't upset the general economy of the Reich too much. But the black-market traffickers who bought for or from the Germans still had their headaches, for German black marketers who had established their businesses in Germany proper were trying to expand into Belgium, where they were undermining the Belgian and the official German black market. These men appealed to the scum of the populace. In the few instances where one of the gang was caught, severe punishment was meted out if he happened to be a Belgian; if he was German, he escaped scot-free.

The Germans kept saying that the reason for the food shortage was that the Belgians refused to deliver their entire food production. Nothing is taken to Germany, they said. This could easily be proved by the production of the ration figures, and this proof will be given, they said, "after the war."

When war broke out, only 133,434 acres of Belgian

soil were used for crops of industrial value such as colza (or rape), beets and hops. The German National Agricultural Corporation, in order to obtain more fats, ordered the farmers to increase the rapeseed production. It required enormous vigilance on the part of the Germans to see that this order was carried out, for the Belgian peasant realized that rape is a poison for his soil, already exhausted by intensive exploitation during the last three years. The Germans insisted and threatened, but the final results were no more fruitful here than was the case with their other endeavors in Belgium. The Nazis promised the population that an increase in the rapeseed harvest would result in an increase in fat rations. When the production was well under way, the Nazis confessed the impossibility of fulfilling their promise.

Then the underground took matters in hand and inaugurated a scorched-earth policy which is unique in the annals of Belgium. "The battle of the colza" was waged in accordance with the best examples set by the Russians. Crops were systematically set on fire; farms of obstinate or collaborationist farmers went up in flames. According to one of the Quisling papers, *La Légia:* "The number of fires has been steadily increasing for over a month now. The sky is filled daily with the glow of flames." In dozens of places the harvest was ruined either by fire or other methods. Colza burned in Walloonia, flax in Flanders. In some places, the saboteurs disarmed the rural guards in German service, forced them to cut the rape and afterward set it on fire. Wheat fields were dealt with in the same way. In the village of K—— a group of Quislings volunteered to guard the fields. One night a gun battle took place, and the Quislings were overpowered. The saboteurs, after having forced them to cut the grain and destroy it, took away their clothes and drove them naked into the woods. In the morning the Quislings came to the town and begged the peasants for clothes. None helped them, and the Germans had to come to their aid.

The Nazi press complained bitterly about all this. It was infuriated by the fact that the underground and the population of Belgium closely followed the advice of the Belgian authorities in London, and that the sabotage effectively succeeded in hitting the Huns where it hurt them most. An issue of the *Journal de Charleroi* wailed: "Raiding a field apparently deserves little notice any more. Pillaging a farm has become a small matter. To terrorize the country is of no importance either. It seems to be of no concern that crime is accepted as a habit and transforms a peaceful country into a flaming hell."

A flaming hell. Such seemed to be the exact picture of the Belgian countryside at that moment. It was one of the loveliest, most prolific, most enchanting spots of western Europe—the very symbol of fertility, peace and riches. For some time the heroes of the underground transformed this fruitful farmland of Europe into a veritable inferno. But the fires were not kindled by these brave and obscure men. The flames first started in the perverted heart of a megalomaniac and in the minds of millions of his followers who have made of the world a sight which even Dante would have hesitated to describe.

V

BELGIAN
"IMPERIALISM"?

1.—Kabambary

THE ROMAN EMPEROR VESPASIAN IS CREDITED WITH THE saying that money has no odor. For this pronouncement and for several other reasons, he is considered a disreputable character.

It is quite certain, however, that if all of us realized the sum of misery and human sufferings which have inevitably preceded our enjoyment of a number of modern commodities, we should feel a good deal worse than, spontaneously and righteously, we want the cynical Vespasian to do.

There was a time, little more than half a century ago, when people amassed great wealth through buying and selling ivory, a merchandise that has no smell either, but the background of this wealth was filled with such horrors that finally the civilized world could stand it no more. It was the privilege of the Belgians to stamp out a regime of terror and brutality, the like of which had seldom been seen. They wiped this shame from the face of Africa, about fifty years ago, when they finally defeated the Arab slave traders on January 24, 1894, at Kabambary.

The entire Upper Congo region, a territory equal to all of the United States east of the Mississippi, was at that time completely in the hands of hundreds of roving bands and plundering murderers, prowling in all directions and robbing the country of its ivory and of its manpower. From the Island of Zanzibar, the Arab traders went into the Congo, and for mere trinkets bought the ivory tusks from the natives. But once the Arabs got hold of fire-arms, they did not bother any more to negotiate—they just took what they wanted, killing the natives and stealing the ivory.

For decades they spread terror and desolation in Central Africa, which they alone knew well. In their search for tusks, they not only destroyed ruthlessly the great herds of elephants which roamed in the African plains and woods, but they found that their trade could not go on if they did not have the collaboration of the natives. They used them as carriers on their long treks through darkest Africa, and those who succeeded in reaching the East Coast were shipped to Zanzibar and sold as slaves on that island. More than 30,000 Negroes per year were thus enslaved, and those 30,000 represented only a small percentage of the large number the Arabs captured and forced into servitude. It has been calculated that for the 30,000 who survived the ordeal, about 120,000 others had to die on the road.

An eyewitness described an Arab caravan as follows:

As they filed past we noticed many chained together by the neck; others had their necks fastened into the forks of poles about six feet long, the ends of which were supported by the man who preceded them. The neck is often broken as the slave falls in walking. The women, who were as numerous as the men, carried babies on their backs in addition to a tusk of ivory on their heads. They looked at us with suspicion and fear, having been told that white men always desired to release slaves in order to eat their flesh, like the Upper Congo cannibals. It is difficult adequately to describe the filthy state of their bodies; in many instances not only scarred by the cut of the chikote (a piece of hide used to enforce obedience), but feet and shoulders were a mass of open sores, made more painful by the swarms of flies which followed the march and lived on the flowing blood. They presented a moving picture of utter misery, and one could not help wondering how many of them had survived the long tramp from the Upper Congo, at least 1,000 miles distant.

The witness asked the Arabs what they did to the slaves who became too ill to travel. "Spear them at once," was the reply. What did they do to the mothers who became too weak to carry both child and ivory? "We spear the child and make her burden lighter. Ivory first, child afterwards."

The most notorious of all the Arab traders was a colorful old scoundrel named Tippo-Tip. According to some, that name meant "Gatherer of wealth," but another story goes that it was an onomatopoeic reproduction of the sound of the guns he used on the natives. Other traders were significantly called "the Locust" and "the Finisher." The most sinister of them all went by the name of Bitter-as-Bile.

Several times Tippo-Tip made long excursions into the Congo, once staying more than five years away from home, leaving everywhere on his passage a trail of devastation and death. Among the savage tribes of the Upper Congo he occasionally and very successfully played politics. He enlisted the assistance of the Manyemas, a cannibal tribe, by promising them that they would be entitled to eat the bodies of another tribe he was going to attack. Cannibalism was so widespread at the time that when it was nec-

essary to inform Tippo-Tip's son Sefu of the death of one
of his lieutenants called Mohara, his man broke the news
gently to him by saying, "A few days ago we ate Mohara."
Tippo-Tip once declared to a white man, "I do not simply
hinder; I destroy." In his period living man was considered "the currency of Africa." Unbelievable acts of mass
cruelty were committed by this man, who to Europeans
was always the most charming and urbane of hosts.

The Belgians understood from the beginning that the
ivory trade and slavery were intimately connected, and
that no civilizing influence in the Congo could endure if
they did not first of all destroy the Arab power in Central
Africa.

In 1892 the Manyemas, incited by Tippo-Tip, revolted.
On March 15, 1892, the Arabs murdered in cold blood a
Belgian agent named Hodister and his ten white compan-
ions. They burned down several Belgian settlements in
the Upper Congo, and for a while it looked as if the Belgian power in that sector was on the verge of a complete
collapse. All the allies of Tippo-Tip took the offensive. A
Negro chief, Ngongo-Lutete, who had allied himself with
Tippo-Tip, went on the war path too. The great leader's
son, Sefu, captured two Belgian lieutenants, Lippens and
De Bruyn, and kept them as hostages, finally killing them.

The Belgian situation was in the hands of a young officer, Georges Dhanis. Dhanis' army, although numerically
inferior to the Arab forces, attacked. He had only seven
Europeans under his command, and three hundred and
fifty regular troops, but he possessed a 7-5 Krupp gun,
which was to play an important role in the campaign, not
only with its bullets, but also by its noise. In several battles he defeated the savage tribes. For years the fight

went on, the adversaries sometimes using Homeric ruses to deceive each other, both groups constantly increasing in numbers until at one time the Arabs put about 60,000 men in line. Dhanis relentlessly chased his enemies, defeating them one by one, but he also suffered reverses. Even in January, 1894, the outcome of the campaign was far from certain. On January 24, however, Dhanis succeeded in destroying an important stronghold of the Arabs in Kabambary. He shot off his Krupp gun and blew up the Arab armory. Thousands of Arabs were captured, and the slave traders realized that at last their empire was definitely crumbling. They disappeared from Central Africa.

The Congo natives who fought in the Belgian ranks had displayed great loyalty to the Belgians and had clearly understood that their future was at stake in the fight against the Arabs. A number of Belgian agents had been massacred by the slave traders and their allies. Many a Belgian officer lost his life in the four-year-long campaign.

Georges Dhanis was made a baron by King Leopold II. He had freed an immense territory from the scourge of slavery. He had made possible for millions of Negroes a peaceful life and the opportunity of developing themselves as civilized beings.

In 1903, Henry M. Stanley, the explorer, appraised the Belgian anti-Arab campaign in these words: "In a limited number of years the King of the Belgians put an end to the horrible Arab slave trade. I do not think there is another sovereign living who has done as much for humanity as Leopold II."

2.—*"By Their Fruits Ye Shall Know Them"*

THE PHYSICISTS TELL US THAT IN THE RELAM OF MATTER nothing is created and nothing goes to waste. Until they change their minds one should believe them. But in the realm of sentiment there is evidently a terrible waste going on. A tremendous amount of pure, generous feeling is spent on causes which prove not to be worth while, and very often people display this generosity on a mere impulse, without stopping to check the facts. Possibly this waste is just apparent, as it is in nature, but no reasonable explanation has yet been given for the fantastic futility of many of our sentimental and intellectual impulses, for the enormous waste of feelings that so often fill this world with disorder and chaos. One thing, however, is clear, although it sounds paradoxical and contradictory in its very terms: in order to love well—an idea at least—one should love wisely. While love for a person is accentuated by mystery, love for an idea should be actuated by knowledge.

All liberals—and few people would dare to say that they are not liberals—love the undeveloped population of Africa. In Belgium the missionary tracts call the Negroes "our black brothers" (which is better than calling them "colored," for they might some day consider things from their standpoint and call us "discolored people"). The African people are loved, and when the liberal defenders of these Negroes want to prove their generous feelings, they argue that the white man has brought nothing to the blacks but misery and hardships. Invariably someone will sum up the whole situation by saying that all the Negroes got out of their contact with the whites was alcoholism, tuberculosis, and syphilis. Nobody will question such a forceful and dramatic statement.

Have the whites introduced alcoholism among the natives in the Congo? Anybody who has set foot on African soil knows that the aborigines did not wait for the white man to get drunk. They even spent a good deal of their time getting "soused." They took and still take their drinking seriously. In the Congo they imbibe either the heady *malafu* or palm wine, or the *pombe,* which is made out of rice and maize. No political transaction takes place between chiefs, no ceremony of any kind is held, no new moon rises above the palms, without big parties being organized, consisting essentially of dancing and drinking. When the social tom-tom says that "a good time was had by all," it means that everyone was, as the poet says:

> In a stupor sent
> By booze of more than two per cent.

The natives were and still are good drinkers, and although the white man's firewater is forbidden them, and white men who sell European liquor are first jailed and then expelled from the Belgian Congo, the natives had and still have all that is necessary to indulge in one of man's many means of killing his sorrows or augmenting his joys.

A Presbyterian minister, Mrs. J. L. Kellersberger, who has passed a good deal of her well-spent life in the Congo, wrote as follows about the Negroes' health standards before the arrival of the white man:

> Ignorance and disregard of infectious disease, before modern medicine intervened, caused the death toll to reach appalling numbers. The death rate became greater than the birth rate and the African was known as a dying race. Drinking cups, cooking utensils, and community pipes were the property of all. Polluted water from any source was freely used, the muddier the better, for clear water, in their opinion, was not strong enough. They bathed the feet first, next the face, then the teeth, and afterwards drank the remaining drops of the same water.

It should cause little astonishment, therefore, that the clinical photographs brought back from Africa by European doctors are among the most horrible things one can see. The Negroes do not suffer to any great extent from any malady the Europeans imported into their country. They fell victims of the terrible local endemic diseases: sleeping sickness, dysentery, leprosy, malaria, smallpox and venereal disease.

Before the Belgians took charge, the sicknesses were "cured" by witch doctors, or were combated by some hocus-pocus rooted in old traditions. The antics of the witch doctors were certainly more impressive and colorful than the cold efficiency of modern medicine, but it did not take long for the natives to observe that the results achieved by huge menacing masks and potions of pulverized birds' tongues were smaller than those attained by the white "sorcerers." Practically all of the 4,000 missionaries have taken up medicine in some way or other. For their charges they have organized hospitals, dispensaries and maternity centers. The big companies assure their workers a standard of hygiene unapproached in many civilized countries. Institutions of Louvain and Brussels Universities carry on medical research and field work. A state foundation called Foreami sets up health centers for entire regions and leaves only when conditions are esteemed satisfactory enough for the health service to be turned over to the regular state organizations; and, finally, the Government Health Service administers eight huge hospitals, thirty-six ordinary hospitals and three hundred and eight-three dispensaries.

Although the Belgian regime in the Congo has received the highest praise from all observers for decades now, many people have feared that under the strain of war conditions, in order to increase production, the authorities would revert to methods which are considered typical of capitalistic exploitation and neglect the welfare of the natives. They forget that King Albert, coming back from an extensive tour in the Congo, said these wise words: "The greatest wealth of the Congo is its population." It is with no little pride that the Belgian Congo today can claim that not only did the war not interfere with the natives' health service, but that more has been done in this field since 1939 than ever before.

Among a population of about 14,000,000 Negroes there are but 40,000 whites. Over 10 per cent of the latter have been mobilized, an enormous figure, taking into consideration the fact that the white population of the Congo is limited to people whose presence is indispensable there. The medical staff of nearly three hundred and fifty doctors, pharmacists and dentists was depleted. One out of seven had to leave. Native medical auxiliaries left for other jobs: one in every four walked out.

How did the medical service stand up under these circumstances? In 1939 the Congo Government alone devoted 81 million francs to its medical service; in 1942 the figure ran to 143 million, and in 1944 it went up to 151 million francs (approximately $5,000,000 in prewar value). To replace the absent nurses more female Negro help has been called upon, with the result that the total number of people employed by the Health Service has been increased rather than diminished.

The results of this policy are extremely encouraging. The proportion between births and deaths in certain cases has been greatly improved. In the capital, Leopoldville, the trend of population figures was especially good. This is particularly interesting because Leopoldville brings together a rather large Negro community of people of many different races. These people are cut off from their racial environment, and much has been said about the fact that, being "on the loose," they lost their good native characteristics and acquired all the vices of the whites. Apparently their reactions are not so bad after all.

In 1942 the number of medical consultations received by the natives was 18,500,000, for a population of about 15,000,000 people. While in 1939 52,000 Negroes were hospitalized, the figure in 1942 rose to 77,000. Operations, of which there were 36,000 before the war, rose to 38,000. While in 1939 18,000 natives were assisted in childbirth, in 1942 more than 29,000 were attended. It should be noted, of course, that these figures show the achievements of the Belgian Administration in only one field of social welfare; similar results have been obtained in the field of education and other social activities.

The Governor-General of the Congo, Mr. Pierre Ryckmans, made it clear that whenever the question of colonial possessions is put before the world, it will be of little avail to claim the antiquity of one's title of possession but, as in the Gospel, those in power will be asked, "What have you done with your talents?" Belgium need not fear that day. She can refer to the facts and the figures as well as to the consensus of the most critical observers.

3.—On Imperialism, True or False

IT IS NATURAL THAT THE PEOPLE OF THE UNITED STATES, having felt what it means to be a colony, and having fought bravely to sever themselves from the oppression of the motherland, spontaneously consider the idea of colonization as taboo and consistently give that term an unpleasant implication it has nowhere else in the world. The same unfavorable connotation accompanies the words "empire" and "imperialism." Ever so often speakers and authors interested in postwar plans (and who isn't?) ask the questions: Is Belgium an imperialist country? Will Belgium renounce imperialism? Will Belgium give the Congo back?

Humanity, among its noblest dreams, has always contemplated the Utopia of a world empire, an organization that would establish universal order and global peace under one single ruler. Such was the ambition of Alexander the Great who, blessed with scarcely twenty-one years, was discouraged at not having any new, worth-while lands to conquer. He found that there was nothing more to be done in the world, and it was too early to take up stamp collecting, to which there positively is no end. The Romans had the same aspirations as Alexander and felt that, as Pliny has it, "Rome was chosen by the providence of the gods to render even heaven more glorious, to unite the scattered empires of the world, to become in short the mother country of all nations of the earth." What Charlemagne and Napoleon attempted along the same line was but a poor imitation, and gradually the idea of the empire began to shrink. No longer did people think of it as a world union, but they felt that there could be several empires of more or less territorial importance. So they became imperialists.

In the nineteenth century it was rather elegant to proclaim oneself an imperialist. It gave an impression of daring and vision, of a muscular conception of life. If, in addition, one was able to quote a few lines from Kipling's jingle-jangle jingo poems about far-flung battle lines, or a line or two from Theodor Körner's bombastic appeals to the Lord of Battles who was supposed to be some kind of a specialist in German service, one could be assured of a pretty good standing in public opinion. All that has gone. Few are the people now who would dare lift up their voices to say: "I am an imperialist." It is tantamount to saying, "I am an opium addict," or "I trade in white cargo." For some obscure and no doubt linguistic reason, the prudish *Encyclopaedia Britannica,* up to recent editions, did not even mention the word, although it is currently used in English books; but the *Americana* knows all about it and makes it absolutely clear that imperialism is indulged in on a large scale by the British.

W. K. Hancock, who has written ponderous and excellent books on the British Empire, got into trouble when trying to define this kind of political sin. "In one morning," he says, "I once counted up ten different meanings given to it by ten different authors: to some of them it meant federation between Great Britain and the Dominions, to others it meant 'dominion over palm and pine,' to others it meant the monopoly stage of capitalism, to others it meant the government of primitive peoples. Its connotation was at one time political, at another time economic, at another racial."

We all know that too much, like too little knowledge, is a terrible nuisance and that scholarly people have a way of complicating the simplest issues. Therefore if we resort to the etymological roots of the word "imperialism," we are sure not to go astray: an imperialist is a man who favors the principle or the spirit of empire, who promotes or is devoted to imperial interests. It is a well-known fact that all empires disintegrate, that none of these gigantic undertakings of unification ever acquired durability, and that most empires end with the last breath of their emperor. The fact that at present a few empires still subsist seems to prove that they are not real empires any more, that they probably suffer from the odium of a name which no longer completely covers the idea or the facts.

Imperialism in modern times, except for the now defunct dream of Hitler, does not envisage the control of the universe. That utopian idea has been abandoned: the term applies now "to the national policy which tends toward the expansion of national domination and national ideas over a geographical area wider than that of national boundaries." That American definition makes the United States a potentially imperialist power, however forcefully public opinion rejects the very idea, for the Supreme Court ruled in 1901 that expansion of the United States is not unconstitutional.

The peace-loving countries of the world proclaim in unison that they want no territorial aggrandizement. None of them asks for *Lebensraum,* and since a true imperialist should always be on the alert to grab whatever he may find, it is evident that imperialism has lost the impetus which is its essence, that it has become to genuine imperialism what Postum is to coffee. Imperialism is on the defense: it is asked to renounce, to give up what it acquired. Like the tippler and the loose woman, it is being "saved."

Are the Belgians in need of this particular brand of salvation? When they stepped into colonial history, they came neither to bury nor to praise imperialism: through the genius of their sovereign, Leopold II, they fell heir to a vast undeveloped territory, eighty times the size of the home country, the King's title to it having been recognized first of all by these United States. They accepted the task of developing this enormous land not through any base materialistic calculations—for you cannot accuse a freely elected parliament of such feelings—and the first Belgians to devote their lives to the Congo were brave pioneer soldiers who died in the anti-slave-trade campaign, and missionaries who went there to spend a hard and humble existence in generous devotion to the natives. The heroism of these hundreds of men abundantly outweighs the few excesses committed by some international rascals who maltreated the natives.

For nearly thirty-six years now the Belgians have taken care of the Congo. According to all Americans who, however prejudiced, visited the Congo—not on a Potemkin tour, but freely, and excursioning at random—the work the Belgians have done deserves unmitigated and high praise. Belgium is not an imperialist country: it does not ask for more and more territory. What it has on its hands is more than enough, and it manages to do its job with devotion, brilliance and success.

It does not have to renounce anything. Its government is democratic, its most powerful parties are almost equally liberal-minded. Whatever even vaguely resembles capitalistic exploitation is combated in Parliament with unceasing vigor and alertness. Far from transforming the Congo into a private hunting ground for Belgians, the colonial statute provides for a very widely developed internationalization of this rich territory. The profits do not go in the main to the Belgians; the burdens are all assumed by them, except for the valuable contribution of foreign missionaries.

Should the Belgians give the Congo back? The answer is another question: To whom? Of course we know that Messrs. Renner and Culbertson want us to give it to the Germans, the poor have-nots of Adolf, but that can scarcely be the intention of the generous Americans who ask the above question ever so often. They have better sense than these two apprentice sorcerers of geopolitics.

They want to know if the Belgians are going to give the Congo back to the natives. The least that can be said about it is that there is a far greater chance for that than for the Lenni-Lenapes to get back Manhattan, even if they offered a cargo of genuine rye. There are fifteen million Negroes in the Congo who used to be cannibals. From time to time they have a tendency to resume that diet, solid traditions being respectable and the meat situation being what it is. They lived under feudal conditions, with very little knowledge of democratic ideas: they had, like most primitive people, the cult of force and cunning. If left to themselves, they would revert to their crude methods of tyranny and barbarism. Civilization has reached only a percentage of them; with some it is only skin deep. The Liberian experiment, even under very favorable auspices, has not been a complete success. The Belgians intend to make an unqualified success of what they have undertaken. They know that the Congo natives are capable of rapid development and are gifted in many ways. They will not relinquish the obligations they freely assumed when they adopted the Congo. Their aim is generally to raise the peoples of the Congo through collaboration to self-government.

It takes a number of years to make citizens out of savages. In the meanwhile the Belgians will willingly endure the unjust and inadequate appellation of "imperialists," for they are convinced that they are performing a great task and they will not be deterred from it, either by the ravings of lunatic planners or by the declamations, however generous but ill-guided, of reformers.

VI
BELGIUM IN THE
FUTURE

VI

BELGIUM IN THE
FUTURE

1.—"À Bientôt"

In the first week of September, 1944, eight and a half million Belgians felt on their lips the sweet taste of victory and liberation. They went around singing, shouting and telling each other it was good to be alive again. They greeted the small Belgian army that marched into Brussels, boys who had come from the four corners of the earth to take part in its liberation, some of whom had traversed two continents to continue the fight. They greeted the British, their traditional protectors and allies, and they stared in admiration at the Americans, who in record time had accomplished a military feat unequaled in history. They remembered how America saved many of their countrymen from starvation in the First World War; they knew that American sacrifice and heroism were responsible for the air of freedom they breathe again, for the new life that begins. In their hearts they have said for all time, *Amica America!*

But in that rapture of joy and gratitude, they think of the future, and they have good reasons to do so. They were told something very important about it by the retreating Nazi scum. On September 1 the German radio in Brussels told them four remarkable things:

1) "We shall never rob you."

2) "We shall never pillage you."
3) "Do not show hatred against us or those in your country who worked for us."
4) "One day we shall come back. Till then, *à bientôt.*"

It is difficult in the face of these remarkable statements to remain objective and calm, but in their enormity they throw such a wonderful light on the German mentality that it would be unwise to neglect them, to discard them as the last babblings of clumsy propagandists. They belong to the psychopathic domain rather than to the realm of politics, and as such they prove once more that the case of Germany pertains to the paranoiac and not to the reasonable.

Those who know the Germans—and it should be repeated that most Americans do not, while most Europeans do—have foreseen long ago that on the day when Hitler and his consorts would be forced to their knees, they would start a well-orchestrated, impressive whining campaign. The Germans know that, spontaneously, the Anglo-Saxon feels for the underdog; they know that when the newsreel shows a few whores shorn of their "crowning glory," women who may have betrayed patriots and sent them to death, the American audience does not like the spectacle. They realize that by whining they achieved quite a few results last time, and the campaign is on. Brussels had the honor of the première. There is a lot more to come. For years we shall hear these pitiful tunes, we shall listen to that falsetto siren song, and if it is in the lap of the gods, the world will succumb a second time to the lure of that fat Lorelei from over the Rhine!

But the Belgians will not. Why? Because when the Germans with grotesque solemnity declare, "We shall

never rob you," the Belgians have a real belly laugh.
These gangsters have raised the public debt from 63 billion francs in 1939 to about 140 billion francs in 1943.
They have drained Belgium of 85 per cent of its production and have kept the funds they owe in their clearing-
house in Berlin; they have imposed on scores of Belgian
cities fines of millions of francs in order to punish them
for their patriotic behavior, they have robbed private
homes, libraries of scientists, they have confiscated the
property of Belgians in exile, stolen art treasures, and in
general have behaved like the vulgar looters they are.
They enjoyed those privileges for four years practically
undisturbed and, on the eve of being driven out of Belgium, they stand up, trembling in their stolen boots, and
with a shamelessness never seen before, they have the
nerve to tell their Belgian victims: "We shall not rob
you." To which the Belgians can give but one answer:
"What is there left to rob?"

They say also: "We shall never pillage you!" For four
years they have lived on the fat of the land, letting the
Belgian children starve, shipping the food the Belgians
produced to the Reich, living on rations threefold those
theoretically allotted to the Belgians. They have rendered
Belgian industry subservient. They stole railroad material,
electrical equipment, in fact everything that was not too
hot or too heavy to carry away. According to the dis-
patches of a correspondent who entered Belgium with the
victorious armies, the Germans have shipped endless
streams of truckloads to the Reich in their retreat. When
everything was cleared up, their announcer coined that
wonderful phrase: "We shall not pillage you."

But the orchid in this bouquet is his humble prayer, the

hangman's prayer: "Do not hate us or those who helped us."

There stands the spokesman of those men who in 1940 killed 10,000 women and children on the roads of Belgium, machine gunning them just for fun; of those men who imprisoned more than 12,000 Belgian patriots; who executed hundreds of innocent hostages; who massacred the people of Deynze; who abducted 500,000 men and women to slavery in German factories; who stole the coal out of Belgian mines and the bells out of the churches; who insulted every decent man and woman in the country—and their authorized spokesman has one little request when leaving: "Do not hate us!"

And he adds: "Do not hate those who helped us"—the people who betrayed their country, who betrayed their own people, who helped us find the editor or printer of the clandestine press, who told us where patriots were in hiding, who guided us to the caches where a poor family kept some food in reserve, so that we could torture these people and, according to Gestapo usage, kill them. Do not hate the few men or women who helped us round up the Jews and send them to Lublin, so that we could asphyxiate them and take the gold out of their teeth. Please, gentle Belgians, do not hate these kind collaborators of ours!

Do not hate those who destroyed, or rather tried in vain to destroy your institutions, every freedom for which you have fought for centuries, everything that made life worth while. No hate, please, for hatred is not gentle and we are just a people of sausage-eating, music-loving, *gemütlich* beer drinkers, and all you have heard about us is just nasty propaganda from Wall Street capitalists and British communists.

One could dismiss all this and say: Let the maniac rave, he fears for his hide and that is all there is to it, but the final sentence of his speech is such a confession and a warning that it deserves the greatest attention.

This is the second time in a quarter of a century that the Germans have occupied Belgium for four years. They are beaten and they know it. The strength of the whole free world is hurled against them, and their game is up. Will they at this moment of the *Götterdämmerung* understand that the world cannot be enslaved? No, the only conclusion they draw in Brussels, as in Paris, as in a dozen other cities, is: "We shall come back." We shall come back with a new edition of the Gestapo, of our gas chambers, of our moronic philosophy, of our arrogance and brutality.

If there is anything the Belgians may be grateful for to the Germans, it is for this warning: "*À bientôt.*"

The horrible truth is that they will be perfectly right, if we treat them again as we did in 1918, if we consider them as normal human beings, if we do not use the sword and nothing but the sword on those who twice took to it. In this supreme hour of the war there is but one watchword: *Delenda Germania!* Cut it into four or eight or twenty pieces, whatever you want, but do not take the risk of standing one day before your children, white with shame and remorse, and having to tell them: "They told us they would come back and, thanks to our foolishness, our weakness and our fair play, they have done so."

2.—*One Step Toward a Better Europe*

THOSE PEOPLE WHO DO NOT KNOW GEOGRAPHY ARE learning very rapidly during this war, but one cannot blame them if at times they are somewhat bewildered. For instance, they knew about the existence of Holland and Belgium, but now they hear about the Low Countries or the Low Lands and also about the Netherlands, and they have a hard time keeping them apart. When they have understood that by Low Countries are meant both Belgium and Holland, although these are separate political entities, that the Netherlands mean only Holland and not Belgium, they are confronted with another problem: the inhabitants of the Netherlands who are called either Dutchmen, Hollanders or Netherlanders speak Dutch, that much one knows. One suspects that it is not the same language as Pennsylvania Dutch, which is German mixed with bad English grammar.

Having progressed that far in the linguistic labyrinth, they hear that not all Belgians speak French but that the majority of them speak Flemish. Then again they are told that Flemish is Dutch and that the official Belgian documents are published both in French and in what is officially called Netherlandish, which is Dutch and which is Flemish. At this point they may lose confidence in their book knowledge and consult a Dutchman (Hollander or Netherlander) and ask him if the Flemings speak Dutch. He may answer, "Yes, in a way!" They may consult a Belgian-Fleming and ask if he speaks Dutch and the answer may be, "I earnestly try to."

To save the poor student of geography from going berserk, someone must stand up and tell him that Flemish is to Dutch what American is to English, or—not to make it too plain at once—the reverse, that the difference between the language of Flanders and that of Holland is approximately the same as that between Mr. Churchill's and Mr. Roosevelt's English, a matter of vocabulary and pronunciation; lift for elevator and pavement for sidewalk, etc., etc. Once the newspaper reader has survived this information and got hold of the clues, he may proceed without danger on the road to further knowledge.

He will find out that the Belgians and the Dutch have a great deal in common, although they are in many respects very different. Up to the end of the sixteenth century they constituted one single country, the seventeen Provinces of the Low Countries which belonged to Spain. All of them revolted against the Spanish regime: the issue was freedom of religion, which meant at that time simply freedom, at least at the outset. Human folly being as it is, immense and incurable, once the fighters for religious freedom attained their object, they started persecuting those who did not adhere to their doctrines, just as a century later the brave men who, on account of their convictions, had come to the wilderness of America used to pester those who did not worship exactly as they did. (It is all very discouraging, but it is wearing off!) When the Spanish reconquered the Southern Netherlands, they restored Catholicism; when they had to give up reducing the Northern Provinces, they were forced to make their peace with these "heretics," who were aggressive Protestants.

From then on till 1814, Holland took the high road to prosperity and riches, while Belgium took the low road to provincialism and mediocrity. Holland became a great nation; Belgium became a more or less neglected outpost of Spain, later on of Austria, and, finally, of conquering France. When the Allied countries had at last broken down the Adolf of their day, Napoleon, they decided to reunite under the Dutch king the seventeen provinces of Charles V and to join Belgium and Holland together.

It did not work out very well, mainly on account of administrative blundering by a well-meaning but very conservative monarch, and to the astonishment of Europe the Belgian revolt against the Dutch regime in 1830 became a success.

The Belgian revolution proved one historical fact—that although people may have a common historical tradition, a common language and a lot of common interests, two centuries of separation create a distance which leaves practical and psychological results. Different institutions influence peoples differently. Above all, the difference in religion between the two countries was instrumental in creating an atmosphere in Holland which could not be likened to the Belgian atmosphere. A century ago the influence of religious thinking on social and political life was certainly far greater than it is now: it was a determining factor in the Dutch-Belgian conflict. The Dutch regarded the Belgians as easygoing, bigoted papists; the

Belgians looked on the Dutch as sour heretics. The Belgians were profoundly influenced by the French outlook on life, the Dutch more by the English and by the lessons they had derived from their own extraordinary achievements on the sea and in the colonies. The Belgians, although most of them were of Dutch stock, had a lot of "Latin" in their character; the Dutch abhorred this apparent flightiness.

All that was one hundred and fourteen years ago and, since then, a lot has changed. Religious differences no longer set nations against each other, men are no longer ready to fight for or against the doctrine of predestination. They fight for their interests and for their civil freedom.

In the last hundred years the Dutch and the Belgians have discovered that—their quarrel being settled—a great number of elements in their respective economies were bound to bring them closer together. Neither of them was bloodthirsty or wanted to avenge anything. There was some bickering from time to time, but it was without consequence. Holland and Belgium found out that they were both small countries of about the same size, as to territory and population, and that they were at the mercy of their neighbors and apt to become buffer states between conflicting interests. They both had colonial empires to protect and care for. Spiritually they enriched each other. Flemish writers learned a great deal from the formal perfection of Dutch letters in the last century, and when Flemish literature experienced a new blossoming, it greatly profited Dutch writing. In recent years there was less distance between Dutch and Flemish letters than there was between French writers and French-writing Belgian authors. The latter had always to contend with a great and productive literary activity; the Flemish authors met the Dutch as perfect equals.

But the main element of rapprochement was the fact that both countries understood how the combination of their economic assets could lead to very interesting results: they were competitors as far as maritime trade was concerned. Both had their commercial hinterland to a great extent in Germany. The ports of Rotterdam and Antwerp sometimes looked askance at each other, each trying to snatch traffic from the other, but after all, that was a traditional procedure which only an earthquake could alter. The competition of two great ports could never lead to the decadence of one or the other: they were doomed to stand each other and to compete.

Economic rapprochements are never based on similarity, but on contrast. For more than thirty years, therefore, groups of businessmen have tried in Belgium and in Holland to establish greater intimacy between both countries because they understood that the mainly agricultural character of Holland's economy would be a complement to the highly industrialized Belgian economy. They had the vision of a group of seventeen million people, located in the most interesting part of Europe, defending their common interests unanimously, making cultural and economic contacts among themselves easier, transforming the Meuse-Rhine-Scheldt delta into an economic unit which, together with the Grand Duchy of Luxembourg, already linked to Belgium in a customs union, would be an impressive and respectable ensemble.

Efforts to that end had failed repeatedly on account of a number of secondary factors. But the common dangers of 1939–1940 brought forth a common political action on the part of Queen Wilhelmina and King Leopold. Together, expressing the will of their peoples, they appealed to the nations of Europe to save peace and they offered their good services. Both Belgium and Holland were engulfed in the German avalanche of 1940. Common suffering and the realization that their fate in Western Europe reposes on solidarity and not on strife resulted very recently in the conclusion of a customs union between Holland and Belgium. It had already existed between Belgium and Luxembourg since 1921, to the satisfaction of both parties. It is temporary in character—because of the war situation. It had been preceded by a monetary agreement between the two nations.

The significance of these agreements for the three parties concerned is not to be underestimated, but they are also of great interest for the rest of the world. Belgians and Dutchmen are known as realistic and practical people. By what they have done, they clearly point the way to a regional reorganization of Europe which will improve economic conditions and which will make international relations safer and sounder.

3.—*Return of the Good and Faithful Servants*

On September 8, 1944, several hundred Belgian officials and refugees stood in Eaton Square, London, cheering a small group of men who were stepping into automobiles ready to take them to an airfield: after four years of exile the Belgian government was flying back to its liberated capital. Belgian flags fluttered in the brisk English September air; the crowd was excited; there were lots of handclasping and claps on the back and shoulders, and, as the Negro story has it, "everybody know everybody else and everybody mighty important."

The Prime Minister, asked for a statement by the press, said simply: "This is the happiest day of my life." Other members of the party wept. In an hour and a half they would reach the goal they had been longing for for four painful years. It sounded incredible, but the airplanes with the Belgian colors on their hulls were waiting on the field: the incredible was going to happen. The wall of cement and steel between their country and Great Britain had crumbled: they were going to be home in an hour and a half.

They were to fly over the Flemish coastline, still partially in enemy hands, to see the light yellow fringe of the beaches, the few undulating dunes, the sturdy towers of the medieval churches along the coast. A few moments later they would see among the neat patterns of the small wheatfields that jewel of history and architecture, Brugge (Bruges). They would have a glimpse of Ghent's belfries and castles and then the plane would take them over the rolling Brabant countryside Breughel used to paint, to Brussels, its lovely Market Square, its venerable cathedral, its ponderous Law Court, which the Nazis had put to fire. The last rays of the evening sun would fall on the thousand hothouses of Hoeylaert where thick, savory grapes were ripening; the glass would cast a blinding reflection as if it were a welcome home.

They must have been silent when the motors slowed down and the planes, with that unique exhilarating feeling of gliding, winged earthward. Silent with gladness and unspeakable joy, silent also with the consciousness of having done their arduous, exhausting duty to the full. One of them had lost two of his young boys in a train accident; one of them had lost two of his sons in combat, the third one fighting on. All of them had been separated from their families and friends. One of them had left his wife and ten children in the hands of the enemy. All had had reason to fear that the Germans would take revenge on their wives and children for whatever they might do or say in London. And besides there was the human angle: four years of separation alter people. There is that wise American poem that says: "It's not your absence that I fear, but your return," . . . not the dangers that you may encounter en route, "but words you may *not* say in greeting."

These men were politicians. Many people have come to use this term in a depreciatory sense. They are wrong. Of course when the politician corresponds to his caricature, he is a despicable character, but so are the butcher, the lawyer or the grocer, if we think of them in the terms the cartoonist uses to stress the abuses of these professions. There are good and bad politicians. It is possible that there are no excellent politicians, just as there are, according to French wisdom, "good" marriages but no "delectable" ones.

Politics is a profession like any other; it has a technique and a number of handicaps. Like any other profession, it deforms the man who is devoted to it: the glass blower overexerts his lungs; sometimes the politician does as much to his mind. But more than anybody else the politician, in difficult times, has a chance to achieve greatness. The histories, simplifying issues and, if need be, inventing beautiful catchwords, cite many instances of declamatory political greatness, but present history shows that all that is but literature, that greatness is seldom achieved in a moment, that it has something to do with time, and that occasional historical words are only the typical expressions of a long, patient evolution.

History alone will determine whether these men were great or whether their smallnesses outdid their latent greatness, but it is already certain that all of them had that permanent quality of patient endurance which made them deserving servants of the national community.

They belonged to a government of national union, bringing together representatives of the three great traditional parties—the Catholics, the Liberals, and the Socialists. In 1940 the two houses of Parliament had charged them to pursue the war to a victorious end. They had known dark and somber days; they may have doubted, but they never failed. Burying their differences of opinion, smoothing over the more angular aspects of their characters, which the war had a tendency to increase, they lived in harmony and they co-operated perfectly for four years.

They were a fair sampling of the Belgian population: typical Walloons like the Prime Minister, Pierlot, born in a small village of the Ardennes forest; like the Minister of Information, Delfosse, a native of valiant Liége; typical Flemings like Mr. De Schrijver, Minister of the Interior, born in Ghent, the most personal and stubborn Flemish city of Flanders; like Mr. De Vleeschauwer, the Minister of Colonies, a husky representative of Flemish peasantry; like Mr. Balthasar, a fighting Socialist deputy from Ghent; and finally there were two natives of Brussels, who are neither fish nor flesh, but a mixture of both —Mr. Spaak, the Minister of Foreign Affairs, and Mr. Gutt, the Minister of Finance, who have in common that art of living typical of Brussels which both Flemings and Walloons, hampered by their romantic temperaments, acquire only with difficulty.

None of them was a demi-god; none of them thought he was. They were human beings all the time and, fighting against terrible odds, they put up in London a governmental administration that was cohesive and efficient. Of course, it was imperfect in some details, mainly on account of insufficient personnel, but good will made up for deficiencies, and complete devotion for inadequate machinery.

For four years these men represented Belgium in the free world. All of them, in the First World War, had been soldiers, had spent years in the trenches or in prison camps. This time they were on another front line, that of Belgium's position in the world. The Allies had recognized them, the Belgians outside Belgium had been loyal to them, the Belgian underground had listened to their orders and applauded their actions. They had done what the Belgian people expected them to do.

When they arrived in Brussels they were cheered by the people, and every Belgian knows that before cheering a minister, a Belgian thinks it over at least twice! They took energetic measures from the beginning, dismissing all collaborationist officials, rebuilding the administrative structure of the nation. They proclaimed their determination to rebuild the country, to insist on the liberation of King Leopold, and to pursue the war.

After a few days in the liberated capital, while fighting was still going on in parts of the country, they already knew that the Belgians are more united than ever and they had the feeling that their long and painful labors had been recompensed by a welcome that expressed warmth and gratitude.